*The Last Lions of Africa*

'*The Last Lions of Africa* is a gem . . . It takes you on a different journey—more informative and spiritual in the telling than any I have read to date. If you think you know lions already, you are about to take your knowledge to another level. What magic he conjures up for us. A wonderful book packed with lyrical insights on the world's most iconic large carnivore . . . a classic.'—Jonathan and Angela Scott, Presenters of *Big Cat Tales* and founders of the Sacred Nature Initiative

'Vastly important.'—David Quammen, author of *Spillover, The Song of the Dodo* and *Breathless*

'This is a remarkable book. In it are piercing, hard-won stories no one else is telling.'—John Vaillant, author of *The Tiger* and *The Golden Spruce*

'The best book on lions I have read in ages. Thoroughly recommended for all big cat fanatics!'—Brian Jackman, author of *The Marsh Lions* and *West with the Light*

'This wonderful book has an elegiac tone and it shows in convincing detail how unlikely we are to preserve wilderness already in my lifetime.'—Lee Kofman, author of *The Writer Laid Bare*

'Urgent and important. This moving tale with a heroic cast of characters, leonine and human, is a must-read for anyone passionate about wildlife and wild places.'—Tony Park, author of *Last Survivor*

'A moving journey . . . Ham is a beautiful storyteller.'—*Australian Women's Weekly*

'This is gripping, insightful, evocative and ultimately heart-breaking reading.'—Travel Africa

'*The Last Lions of Africa* is much more than a tale about the struggle to save the lion from extinction. What makes it so rewarding and gives it mythic resonance is the way Ham captures the intimate, complex interrelationships between humans—farmers, villagers, hunters, conservationists—and these proud, awe-inspiring beasts.'—*Sydney Morning Herald* (syndicated to *The Age*)

'A gripping campfire story indeed . . . these regal lords of their world are brought vividly to life by this exceptional writer and very brave man.'—*The Chronicle*

'A wake-up call on how close lions are to becoming extinct . . . what cannot be disputed is the incredible lengths Ham went to to tell this important story.'—*The Weekly Times*

'An extraordinary and poignant account of one man's love of the world of lions . . . Through the vivid storytelling, we are enlightened, entertained and become engaged with the fate of these embattled creatures and the surprising ways they might be saved.'—*PS News*

'A fascinating and thought-provoking read about these majestic creatures in peril.'—Booklover Book Reviews

'Richly written in beautifully evocative language, this is a riveting love song to the plight of lions, beautiful and confronting.'—Great Escape Books

A TRUE STORY OF LIFE AND
DEATH IN THE AMAZON

# THE MAN
# WHO
# LOVED
# PINK
# DOLPHINS

ANTHONY HAM

ALLEN&UNWIN
SYDNEY·MELBOURNE·AUCKLAND·LONDON

Allen & Unwin
83 Alexander Street
Crows Nest NSW 2065
Australia
Phone:(61 2) 8425 0100
Email:info@allenandunwin.com
Web:www.allenandunwin.com

A catalogue record for this book is available from the National Library of Australia

ISBN 978 1 76106 551 4

Map by Flat Earth Mapping
Internal design by Post Pre-press
Set in 12.5/17.5 pt Minion Pro Regular by Post Pre-press Group, Australia
Printed in Australia by McPherson's Printing Group

10 9 8 7 6 5 4 3 2 1

*For Marina*

# Contents

## Book Three

Caribbean Sea

Caracas

Port-of-Spain

VENEZUELA

Bogota

Georgetown

SURINAME

FRENCH GUIANA

COLOMBIA

GUYANA

*See Amazon
Basin map*

Quito

ECUADOR

Negro

Amazon

Belém

Moura

Solimões

Manaus

Santarém

B R A Z I L

P E R U

Lima

Reserva Extrativista
Chico Mendes

Xingu
Indigenous Park

BOLIVIA

La Paz

Brasília

Sucre

P A R A G U A Y

PACIFIC
OCEAN

Sao Paulo

Rio de Janeiro

C H I L E

Asuncion

Santiago

URUGUAY

Buenos Aires

Montevideo

ARGENTINA

ATLANTIC
OCEAN

N
NORTH

0                    1000

KILOMETRES

Map produced by **flatEARTH**mapping.com.au
Made with Natural Earth © copyright 2022

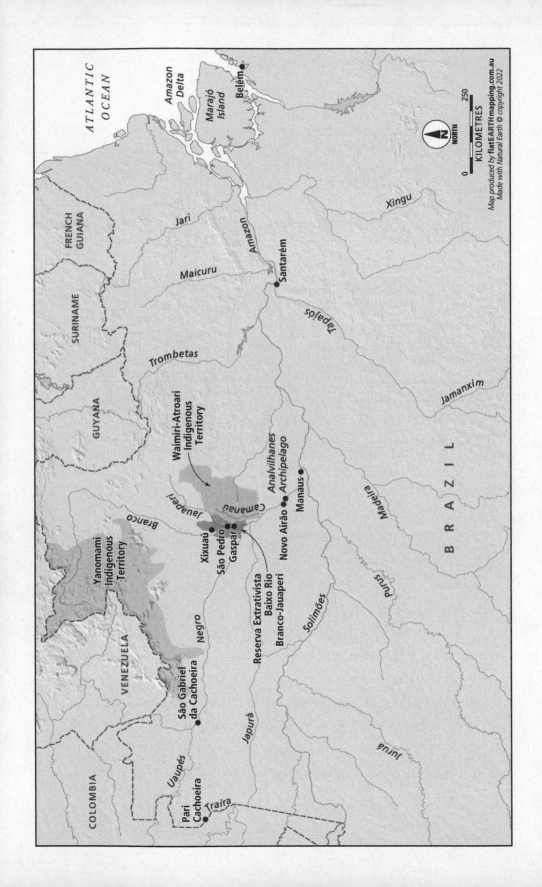

ATLANTIC
OCEAN

Amazon Delta

Marajó Island

Belém

FRENCH GUIANA

Jari

Amazon

Xingu

Maicuru

Santarém

SURINAME

Tapajós

Trombetas

Jamanxim

GUYANA

Waimiri-Atroari
Indigenous
Territory

Analvilhanes
Archipelago

Jauaperi

Camanaú

BRAZIL

Manaus

Branco

Xixuaú

Novo Airão

Yanomami
Indigenous
Territory

São Pedro
Gaspar

Madeira

VENEZUELA

Reserva Extrativista
Baixo Rio
Branco-Jauaperi

Purus

Negro

Solimões

São Gabriel
da Cachoeira

Japurá

Juruá

COLOMBIA

Uaupés

Pari
Cachoeira

Traíra

NORTH

KILOMETRES

0          250

Map produced by flatEARTHmapping.com.au
Made with Natural Earth © copyright 2022

# Prologue

## *2018*

It's difficult when the person who promises to kill you lives just across the water.

This wasn't the first time that someone had threatened Christopher Clark: in the Brazilian Amazon, warnings of one's demise come with the territory. Clark had been in the Amazon for more than three decades. He knew that, out on the frontier where the nearest road can be hundreds of kilometres away, danger can come in many forms. There was little point seeking protection from the local authorities. In Clark's experience, even when you could find them, it was not always obvious whose side they were on.

There was the time when military police wielding machine-guns, their faces hidden behind balaclavas, raided his remote hut at Xixuaú (pronounced *shish-wa-OO*), many miles north of the Rio Negro. Or local politicians would turn up and threaten to burn down his house. And yet, so fluid was the Amazon's tangle of loyalties, so real were the threats, that there were times when the authorities tried to protect him. Marina Silva, who was at the time Brazil's Minister of the Environment, once implored Clark to accept federal police protection. He turned her down because, well, there just didn't seem to be much point. 'The houses here are open,' he told me. 'Even if you've got a couple of police guys, it wouldn't have been at all difficult to kill me.'

Sometimes the threats were thinly veiled rumours that were no less frightening because they were delivered second- or third-hand. 'Everybody was talking about it, saying "They want rid of you" or "They don't want you here",' Clark explained, years later. Just as often, the threats were more explicit, part and parcel of Amazon-style politics. 'You're going to get a bullet in the back,' a local politician once warned him. Even now, Clark knows how easy it would be to eliminate an enemy. 'If I wanted somebody to kill you, I could get it done for hundreds of reais,' he told me.[1] 'Not *thousands* of reais; *hundreds* of reais.'

But this time, the threat was different.

On 17 July 2018, a local turtle hunter named Agostinho da Silva (not his real name) left the village across the lagoon from Clark's house and paddled his canoe to Clark's boat landing. Clark was in Novo Airão, the nearest major town and a two-day journey downriver, at the time. Only Mariana—a local woman, and Clark's cook and family friend—was there. Agostinho shouted at her to leave, told her he was going to set fire to Clark's home. Mariana stood her ground. Agostinho was enraged. According to a police report of the incident, he smashed one of Clark's canoes. He then told Mariana, speaking of Clark: 'The place and hour of his death have been decided!'

Unlike earlier threats, this one was personal, and followed a form well known in these parts. 'It is a chilling tradition in the Amazon,' wrote Andrew Revkin in *The Burning Season*, his account of the murder of Amazon activist Chico Mendes in 1988, 'that the victim is always given notice that his life is scheduled to be taken, as if he were an employee being terminated. An *anúncio*, as such a death notice is called, is not so much a threat as a statement of fact. It is meant to prolong the victim's torment as he waits for the inevitable.'

When news of the threat reached Clark in Novo Airão, he went to the local police station to file a report. Later the same day, as Clark was leaving a local grocery store in town with his adult daughter, Cathleen, a man approached. He got into their car, and told them that he planned to kill them.

When I met him for the first time a few days later, Clark didn't seem to be afraid. Instead, he was annoyed that he had to watch his back yet again. Agostinho was the brother of one of Clark's closest friends, and Clark had helped him generously and often over the years. In the days before my arrival, Clark tried to buy a revolver in Novo Airão, to help defend himself and his family. But he'd been unlucky. A local crime boss had disappeared while in police custody a few weeks before, and those with guns for sale were lying low. Clark was sleeping with a rifle under his bed. He was tired of waiting for danger to come to him. If it came to a shootout, he wanted to fire the first shot.

Clark's time in the Amazon makes for a cracking tale. It's a true drama of the frontier, of Brazil's Wild West. Worthy at times of a Brazilian *telenovela*, it is a story of resilience and danger, of desperate setbacks and remarkable achievements. The little I knew of Clark suggested that he was a flawed hero, a benevolent, modern-day Kurtz with a devoted band of friends and followers deep in a prehistoric jungle many days' journey upriver from so-called civilisation. That was the story I'd come to Brazil to write.

But when I arrived in the Amazon, I knew nothing of threats to Clark's life posed by Agostinho and others. Clark's purpose in the Amazon was serious work: he wanted to save a significant part of the world's greatest rainforest and river system. I was here to write Clark's story. In doing so, I hoped to tell a broader story of the Amazon in peril. I had no intention of becoming part of that story. But soon I had no choice.

Clark's home was a two-day river journey north of Novo Airão. There were no roads where he lived. The river was the only way in or out. It was one of the most remote places I had ever been and, over the days and weeks I spent there, I came to know the wilderness of Xixuaú as a profoundly isolated, wild world, and as a place of rare and beguiling beauty. During my stay, Clark told me his life story and the story of this remarkable place. I revelled in the sheer wonder of it all.

On the night before we were to leave and Clark was to take me back downriver, Clark received a message from a friend. Agostinho had left the village a few days earlier. While no one knew exactly where he was, locals understood that the would-be assassin was lying in wait by the riverbank along the route we planned to take the following day.

'It's probably best if you lie down in the canoe on the way back,' Clark suggested to me drily. 'Just in case. It'll make you a much smaller target. He wouldn't be shooting at you. But from a distance . . .' His voice trailed off. 'From a distance it's impossible for him to maybe not get it wrong.'

How did it come to this? Sometimes writing stories that matter is dangerous. In Clark's case, it's just what happens when you try to save the Amazon.

# Book One

# 1

# Belém

*2018*

Close to where the Amazon empties into the sea, Belém. Of all the Amazon's cities, its second-largest metropolis is surely its most elegant. Belém was Lisbon reborn in rainforest, floated downriver, then attached to a riverbank in the tropics. Washed by tides of slavery and rebellion, seeded by exploration and commerce, this city of neglected pastel-hued warehouses and faded tiled façades whispered intrigue and ruinous decay. Here was a once-beautiful courtesan, long past her prime.

Seen from high on the ramparts of the Forte do Presépio in July 2018, the river at Belém, a branch of the Amazon, flowed wide and muddy brown, more impressive than beautiful. The Portuguese built the fort in 1616, an enduring monument to the notion that those who held Belém somehow controlled the Amazon. Across the vast and impersonal body of water, the far shore, a thin green line, demarcated water from a slate-grey sky. It also separated Belém from the true Amazon, which lay away to the north, beyond the trees. By the water's edge, the wind felt like the ocean's breath, warm, blustery and unimpeded by low-slung riverbanks. *Urubu*—hunched, gaunt black vultures—picked through the evil-smelling rubbish of the old port like faded, high-heeled society belles fallen on hard times. In spite of everything, they stepped carefully through the gathered refuse with a certain elegance.

I was in Belém on my way to see Chris Clark in Xixuaú. His remote hut lay many days' journey upriver. To truly explore the Amazon would take a lifetime. Yet just being here was to glimpse one of our planet's most significant natural realms. The Amazon possesses in its rivers, and in its forests, all of the gravitas that we reserve for places like the Himalaya, the Sahara, outer space and very little else. I was as excited as a child taking first steps.

Belém is the oldest European settlement along the Amazon, but the outside world's fascination with the river predates the city. In February 1500, a caravel[2] under the flag of Spain and the command of Vicente Yáñez Pinzón sailed south through the Atlantic. More than 150 kilometres east of the South American shore, in what appeared to be mid-ocean, Yáñez Pinzón and his crew encountered fresh water flowing east. So far were they from land, and scarcely able to imagine at the time that it might be a river, Yáñez Pinzón named it La Mar Dulce (The Sweet or Freshwater Sea).

The name 'Amazon' owes everything to the vivid imaginations of the Europeans who followed Yáñez Pinzón. Early Spanish and Portuguese explorers who travelled upriver told of tribes led by mighty female warriors. Friar Gaspar de Carvajal, chronicler of a 1542 Spanish-led descent of the Amazon River, wrote:

> We ourselves saw ten or twelve of these women, fighting there as female captains, in front of all the Indian men. They fought so courageously that the men did not dare to run away. They killed any who did turn back, with their clubs, right there in front of us; which was why the Indians maintained their defence for so long. These women are very pale and tall, with very long braided hair wound about their heads. They are very robust and go naked with their private parts covered, bows and arrows in their hands, fighting as much as ten Indian men.

A prisoner told Carvajal that these women warriors had sexual intercourse with men just once a year and kept only their female offspring. They also cut off one breast each, he said, so that they could fire their bows unhindered.

Stories such as these played well to a European audience. They echoed ancient Greek myths of the Amazons, a race of warrior women operating beyond the boundaries of the known world. They were daughters of Ares, the god of war. They fought against Hercules and sided with Troy in their battle with the Greeks. And artists immortalised them, including upon prominent panels of the Parthenon. Like Carvajal's female captains of the forest, the Amazons were feared leaders and soldiers. According to legend, they even burned off their right breasts to better facilitate their ability to throw spears and draw back their bowstrings. For a time, scholars believed that the name derived from the Ancient Greek words *a-mazos*, which means 'without breast'. Etymologists later discredited this explanation, and no credible source has ever produced evidence of women warriors in the forests of South America. Even so, the name stuck.

When it comes to the Amazon, there was no need for exaggeration: its history is an epic worthy of the Greeks. The Amazon once flowed not east but west, all the way into the Pacific. How do we know? Because silt and sediment from South America's east is found deep in the central rainforest, and stingrays in the Amazon are close relatives of those in the Pacific. As the Andes thrust up towards the sky some 15 to 20 million years ago, the river changed direction. Blocked from flowing west, the waters formed a vast inland sea in the heart of what we now know as South America, and the sediment settled as sand. This is why so much of the Amazon has sandy soils to this day. For a time, a ridge in the east known as the Purus Arch hemmed in this sea in the heart of the continent. But as relentless waters flowed down off the Andes watershed, the Amazon washed over and through the ridge, down towards the Atlantic, forever coursing east.

The Amazon begins high in the Andes, in Peru, some 5500 metres above sea level and barely 150 kilometres from the Pacific. In its first 1000 kilometres, flowing east, the river plunges nearly 4800 metres. For the remaining 5700 kilometres, it descends just 700 metres—no wonder it can appear so sluggish. Along its route, it gathers new momentum and volume from the many tributaries that drain into the river's main channel. At its broadest, it is nearly 29 kilometres wide. At times of high water, it is impossible to see the far shore, even from the middle of the river. When and where water levels fall, it can still be 8 kilometres across. As it empties into the sea north of Belém, it bears on its currents one-fifth of all fresh water flowing into the oceans of the world. Close to the river's mouth, an island called the Ilha de Marajó has formed from eight million years' worth of silt and sediment washed down the river. The island is the size of Switzerland, and on maps it resembles a leaky cork. Only in the Amazon can a river island be as large as a country. Yet it is still not large enough to block the river's dramatic entry into the ocean.

Then there are the forests that the Amazon and its tributaries feed. More species live in the Amazon than have existed, ever, in the Earth's four billion years. Despite all that has happened to them, the rainforests of the Amazon still generate one-fifth of the oxygen on earth. One in five of all the world's bird species live here, one-third of its fish. More than 3000 species of freshwater fish swim through the rivers of the Amazon— the vast Mississippi–Missouri river system can muster just 375. David Campbell's *Land of Ghosts*, a lyrical field study of 18 hectares (180,000 square metres) of the rainforests of western Amazonia encountered more than 20,000 individual trees that belonged to around 2000 species. This is more than one-fifth the number of tree species in all of North America. The world's most diverse temperate forest, in Appalachia in the United States, has 158 different tree species. A study found that one 250-hectare (2.5-square-kilometre) plot in the Amazon alone had 414. A single tree studied by scientists was found to shelter 1500 different kinds of insects. Another tree taken at random was home to almost as many species of ant as there are in all of Germany.

Where this wild profusion meets the sea, the Portuguese founded Belém do Pará, building their fort in 1616. The Portuguese empire was capable of extraordinary cultural and architectural achievements. The sophistication of their urban societies spawned a spirit of exploration and an age of scientific discovery. The Portuguese led the world in everything from cartographical innovation to astronomy. But to do so they relied on extraordinary cruelty as they tore down the trees and murdered the local inhabitants.

For the briefest of periods at the start of the Portuguese era in Brazil, colonial settler lived alongside Indian.[3] But before long, on the pretext of Indian resistance, the Portuguese and their foot soldiers nearly wiped out the locals in the area near Belém. They also sent slave traders upriver. Not long after the Portuguese founded Belém, a bishop wrote of how, within a 500-kilometre radius of the city, 'every Indian is at peace and subdued by the Portuguese, whom they fear more than slaves fear their masters . . . In Pará, there were once so many Indians and villages along the banks of its great rivers that visitors marvelled. Now few remain unscathed. The rest have perished, from the injustices to which slave-raiders subjected them.' In 1647, Friar Cristóvão de Lisboa reported that 'when the Indians saw that they were gradually all being enslaved, contrary to all justice and reason, in despair they set fire to their villages and fled into the depths of the forest'. Belém's white population in 1653 was barely 300 people. And yet, one report at the time suggested that the Portuguese killed as many as two million Indians in the decades that followed European settlement at the mouth of the Amazon. It was just the beginning. As John Hemming, the world's leading historian of the Amazon, has written, 'To paraphrase Churchill, rarely in human history has so much damage been done to so many by so few. A few thousand colonists gradually destroyed almost every human being along thousands of kilometres of the main river and its tributaries.'

For nearly a century, Belém was a remote and lawless place. It was a minor outpost left to its own devices far from the halls of power. As happened so often in such places on the frontiers of empire, slave markets stood alongside churches. In 1700, local farmer Plácido José de Souza found a small statue of the Virgin Mary in the mud along a riverbank. He took it home, but the tiny statue kept returning to the place where it had been found. A miracle was declared, word spread, and pilgrims have been flocking to Belém—whose name means Bethlehem in Portuguese—ever since. To this day, every October, fuelled by the fervour and ornate melancholy of old Catholicism, the weeping faithful pull the statue in a carriage through the streets. All the while, thousands clamour and surge to touch or pull the 400-metre-long, 450-kilogram rope.

When French scientist and savant Charles Marie de La Condamine passed through in 1743, he found Belém to be 'a city with well-aligned streets, delightful houses . . . and magnificent churches'. After the 1750 Treaty of Madrid divided the Americas between Spain and Portugal, the Portuguese put their aesthetic stamp upon the city. In 1753, the city fathers commissioned an architect, Giuseppe Landi, from Bologna in Italy, to bring style and beauty and echoes of Lisbon to Belém. Landi was a true Renaissance man. In addition to his architectural prowess, he wrote one of the first natural histories of the Amazon region, and he established a tile-making factory in the city. Later, he fell in love with a local woman, and with the city, where he stayed until his death some four decades after his arrival. By then he had transformed Belém into what John Hemming has called 'the most handsome city in all Amazonia'. His baroque confections remain, including the cathedral on the site where Plácido José de Souza found the statue of the Virgin Mary in 1700. Landi also imported from Asia the mango trees that still provide shade and some respite from the tropical sun along many Belém streets.

Nearly three centuries after Giuseppe Landi's arrival, I sat in Belém's Praça da República. In the shade of a venerable mango tree, João sat down beside me. He was of indeterminate age. 'How old do I look? I am like Belém—I get better with age,' he said, eyes sparkling. He didn't tell me his family name: 'They used to call this place Nossa Senhora de Belém do Grão Pará, but now it's just Belém. I am João. Just João.'

João was silent for a few minutes as he caught his breath. When he spoke, a hint of Belém's melancholy rose in thick Portuguese vowels that were as heavy as the moist, tropical air. Then they, too, subsided, as if nothing could be sustained for long in the stifling heat.

I asked João the secret to knowing Belém. He seemed unsurprised that I should ask. 'Belém is a temptress. But her beauty is only skin deep. Look behind the façades, and she is not what you imagine her to be. Her secrets are dark.' He paused, a smile playing faintly across his lips. 'This, too, has been one of the dark places of the Earth,' João said. When I smiled, he patted my knee: 'I see that you have read Conrad. Very good.' And with that he rose and shuffled away.

Trade, both legal and otherwise, has always sustained the city. It lives on in the waterfront Mercado Ver-o-Peso (the Check-the-Weight Market) where smugglers once mingled with customs officials. These guardians of the port famously took their share as they turned a blind eye to illicit activities. Or, if the circumstances of the day dictated, they levied taxes on cacao, indigo, fish, animal skins and slaves. Belém's veneer of sophistication came crashing down during the nineteenth-century Cabanagem rebellion, when massacres brought the city to its knees. The rubber boom at the turn of the twentieth century revived the city's fortunes, and Belém's population rose from 40,000 in 1875 to more than 100,000 in 1900. Soon, the mansions of wealthy rubber barons added to the elegance of Landi's Belém. Electricity and telephones arrived, and streetcars plied the streets.

Later, long after the decline of rubber, the city settled into obscurity. Like any great port city, Belém was vaguely sordid, slightly dangerous and never quite what it seemed, all in equal measure. When the American writer and naturalist Peter Matthiessen passed through in 1959, he found a city where 'everything is against the law and everything is permitted'.

Through it all, Belém remained a relatively small urban island in a sea of jungle, a mere point of punctuation between Atlantic blues and Amazon greens. In 1848, legendary

English naturalist Alfred Russel Wallace described Belém as 'surrounded by the dense forest'. In the same year another Englishman, Henry Walter Bates, saw in Belém 'the frontier of the great primeval forest . . . which contains so many wonders in its recesses, and clothes the whole surface of the country for two thousand miles [3200 kilometres] from this point to the foot of the Andes'. Bates counted more than 700 different species of butterfly within a radius of an hour's walk of the city centre, compared to just 482 in the whole of Europe. Even more than a century later, in 1959, Peter Matthiessen arrived by boat in a city dwarfed by the rainforest that surrounded it. He noted 'a deep sense of the smallness of Belém, of the hugeness which lies all around it and beyond'.

No longer.

Today, Belém is a city of skyscrapers and 1.5 million souls. More than a million tons of river freight pass through Belém. These include the rainforest's natural riches—timber; soybeans grown on lands where once there were forests; gold, aluminium and iron ore dug from mines on Indian land—that depart the Amazon forever.

While in Belém, at the Parque Zoobotánico, I saw a jaguar, an anaconda and river otters. But the zoo was a sad place. 'Look, a tiger!' a father called to his son at the jaguar enclosure. Children banged on the glass, trying to rouse the anaconda. Adults threw food scraps at the otters. Caged animals here, and the refuse-eating black vultures of the port: these were pretty much all that remained of the Amazon's wildlife for hundreds of miles into the interior. Belém's Indian peoples were also long ago wiped from the map and survived here only in the faces of families who visited the zoo. Denuded land now extended from the city limits, wherever they were, and the introduced mango trees were poor substitutes for the great forests that once adorned the continent from here to the Andes.

As a gateway to the Amazon, Belém was not without charm and intrigue, nor even beauty after a fashion, as long as you squinted into a riverside sunset and held your nose a little.

But this was not the Amazon I sought.

# 2

# Santarém

*2018*

I flew upriver to sultry Santarém. Like so many towns in the Amazon, Santarém was an island in the forest. Roads fanned out from the riverbank in many directions, but few of them remained paved for long. To travel here by road from elsewhere in Brazil meant a days-long expedition on roads that washed away and became impassable for part of the year. Travelling by river was more reliable but equally slow. It took two days to travel upriver from here to the capital of Brazilian Amazonas, Manaus, or downriver to Belém.

In this languid riverside town where very little seemed to happen for much of the day while I was there, the sun bore down upon the population and drove everyone indoors. Those with nowhere else to go waited out the day in the thin shade offered by riverbank trees. The long daylight hours lingered like a searing headache. Time passed slowly in a haze of heat.

It was a city becalmed.

Close to sunset, old men took up their seats around the Praça do Pescador where shabby floor tiles buckled beneath a public telephone shaped like a macaw. Men on motorbikes circled slowly, watched by young women who pretended not to notice the men in the still, steamy air. Shuttered façades faced out across the square towards the river. They gave signs of neither life nor light as the day darkened; they were mere props for the evening set piece of boy meets girl along the waterfront at Santarém. The motorbikes circled one way. The girls circled the other. This passed for entertainment here in the provinces.

The Praça do Pescador, its smell of fish and decay made bearable as the sun lost its sting, drew more and more people until darkness fell and the would-be lovers melted into the crowd and disappeared, lost to assignations that I could no longer see. The whole town then filled the tables out along the jetty, there to enjoy pizzas and caipirinhas as the sun set over the river.

Here at Santarém, the clearwater Tapajós River flows into the main branch of the Amazon. I took a boat out onto the water to see where the two rivers meet. For a time, the blue Tapajós ran alongside the muddy-brown Amazon. A clear line ran down the centre of the main river. Here were two separate rivers fighting for dominance, churning together on their mid-river margins. Downstream the Amazon would win, as it always does.

One of the Amazon's most important tributaries, the Tapajós provides the Amazon with 6 per cent of its flow. It is one of the most beautiful rivers of the entire basin.

The Tapajós rises in Mato Grosso state, where cattle ranching and soybean agriculture on a semi-industrial scale have cleared the forest. In those upper reaches of the Tapajós, the river, like the forest, is itself in danger. Up there, developers plan three dams along the river.

Hydroelectricity provides Brazil with 80 per cent of its power needs but, too often, dams in the Amazon create far more problems than they solve. They threaten unique flora and fauna in the lands that they flood, and imperil the Indigenous communities who live along the river's banks in supposedly protected homelands. The blocking of a river's flow and the flooding of its forests cause fundamental change to riverine ecosystems.

In 2016, *The Washington Post* described the Tapajós as 'one of the last unobstructed tributaries in the Amazon'. It also identified the proposed São Luiz do Tapajós mega dam— which would flood 40,000 hectares (400 square kilometres) of forest—as the next major environmental battle over the Amazon's future. By eliminating rapids, the Tapajós dams such as São Luiz would enable barges filled with soybeans to travel from the farms of Mato Grosso to Amazonian ports. São Luiz would also forever destroy this most beautiful river. Officially on hold since August 2016 when the project lost its licence from IBAMA, Brazil's peak environmental body, São Luiz do Tapajós remains a glint in many a politician's eye.[4]

Until the dam goes ahead, the Tapajós leaves behind its troubles in Mato Grosso and flows north through forest that remains relatively unscathed. Along the way, it marks the border of Amazonas and Pará states. Later, it passes

Fordlândia. This was where the Ford Motor Company brought the idea of a rubber town from the American Midwest to the banks of the Tapajós in the early decades of the twentieth century. Established in 1928, it was, for a time, the Amazon's fourth-largest city, after Belém, Manaus and Iquitos. Provisioned by a company cargo ship that laboured up the Tapajós, Fordlândia had street lighting and swimming pools, cinemas and golf courses. It was supposed to be a shining example of American ingenuity and progress. Ford abandoned Fordlândia in 1934.

On an excursion from Santarém, I found Belterra, Fordlândia's more accessible offspring. Traces of an orderly town survived in the footpaths and managers' cottages with front porches, and in the prim gardens that peered from beneath the encroaching forest. Great snarls of vegetation swallowed rusting hulks of machinery, forlorn and disturbing echoes of another time. In its heyday, Belterra had a population of nearly 10,000 people, and the rubber bosses planted more than 3.5 million rubber trees in the area. Belterra's time passed long ago. Even so, freed from the unrealistic expectations that doomed Fordlândia, at the time of my visit nearby rubber plantations still supported a small population of rubber workers and their families.

Later, in my quest for some glimpse of the Amazon as I imagined it to be, I slept in a hammock on a boat on Lake Maicá. Pink dolphins—Amazon river dolphins—breached otherwise still waters. There were chestnut-fronted macaws and slow-motion sloths. Hoatzins huffed and puffed on an island of reeds. It was a taste.

But Santarém and its people lay just beyond the tree line, and signs of human encroachment were everywhere. Fishing huts lay submerged, and the forest ate away at waterside haciendas. Sluggish river barges chug-chugged along the river's main channel with their cargo of felled timber, bound for the open ocean. It could have been worse. In 2016, Brazil's Federal Court stopped construction of a large grain terminal by the lake.

Nearby, a hideous port facility towered over the river. Global agribusiness corporation Cargill, headquartered in the US, built the port to process its vast soybean crops in 2003. It did so without an environmental impact assessment. The authorities allowed it to operate anyway. The port lay at the end of the BR-163, the so-called Soy Highway, which runs for around 1700 kilometres and may one day carry three million tonnes of soybeans to the port for processing and loading onto ocean-going river vessels. Every soybean exported from here will be grown on land that once was rainforest.

Santarém has been central to this kind of plunder of the Amazon's resources for nearly 150 years. It began in 1876, the year that English trader Henry Wickham loaded 70,000 seeds and saplings from the *Hevea brasiliensis* plant, the tree from which rubber is extracted and refined, onto a ship in the port of Santarém. In the official documentation, Wickham described his illicit cargo as 'academic specimens'. Thus obscured, he sent it downriver and onwards to Kew Gardens in London. From there, the British authorities exported it to their colonies in Malaya and elsewhere. The resulting plantations forever robbed Brazil of its rubber monopoly.

Santarém is now a major hub for the laundering of illegal timber. According to a 2014 Greenpeace investigation, logging trucks leave Santarém during daylight hours. Without any cargo, they travel hundreds of kilometres, crossing the Curuá Una River and on into remote, publicly owned forests south of the city. There they load onto their trucks the timber that has been felled in clandestine logging camps and left by the side of the track, ready for collection. Then the trucks and their drivers wait out the day. Later, under cover of darkness, nearly 100 fully laden trucks return to Santarém every night, creating traffic jams across town as the city sleeps. Back in the city, the ill-gotten timber is comingled with legally harvested wood, or 'warmed' as it's known in the industry. Then customs officials and their agents prepare the necessary paperwork to ensure that the illicit cargo is indistinguishable from timber that has the necessary legal credits. By the time Santarém wakes, the deals have been done and vast timber stockpiles are ready for export to Europe, China, Japan and the US.

I wanted to see what was left of the true forest. A wild-eyed naturalist and guide named Gil Serique took me to the Floresta Nacional do Tapajós (FLONA do Tapajós). Once part of the rubber-tapping domain owned by Gil's family, the FLONA do Tapajós is now among the last stands of rainforest close to Santarém. One minute we were travelling along a road shadowed by fields of soybeans in bright, unnatural greens. The next we were beyond the wall of tall trees and tangled vines, and in a world that bore no resemblance to any place I had ever been. 'One steps through the wall of the tropic forest, as Alice stepped through the looking glass,' Peter Matthiessen wrote in 1961. 'A few steps and the wall closes behind.'

When I first entered the forest, I fell silent. Lianas (vines) cascaded from on high. Great trunks climbed towards the sun and the clerestory-like canopy. In true forest such as this, less than 1 per cent of the sunlight that beats down upon the forest at midday reaches the forest floor. There was beauty none-theless in the dappled light, filtered as through windows of stained glass. Giant *samaúma* trees—also known as ceiba or kapok—rose almost 100 metres into the whorl of vegetation at the forest's summit. The alcoves formed by the *samaúma* buttresses, tens of metres tall, looked like they belonged in some vast Gothic cathedral. With its nunbirds and Jesus lizards, the Amazon lends itself to such comparisons.

It was a strange kind of cathedral, in its own way macabre. When a cloud passed across the sun, the forest light turned gloomy, even sepulchral. Up above, the glimpsed face of a capu-chin monkey, barely discernible through the leaves, flitted into focus as if imprisoned in some high tower. Down below, on the forest floor, the pale faces of dead leaves peered from tannin-stained puddles, like lost souls trapped in the ghastly transparent tombs of Purgatory. Small butterflies—white, yellow and lime-green—clustered, as if attending mass on another small puddle, then rose to fill the air like confetti when disturbed.

In places, scarified trunks of rubber trees with their strict hierarchy of contour-like lines could have been signposts to some antediluvian jungle civilisation. Elsewhere, the forest was a wild tangle of foliage that joined in an exuberant mael-strom of green where the line between darkness and light was sometimes difficult to discern. For the most part, a colossal silence reigned. Every twig crack startled. There were sounds— far-off chirrups and the occasional crash as a squirrel monkey fled through the higher branches. But these seemed to come from the beyond, from places concealed behind the impenetrable wall of trees. There were so many mysteries here, so many things I could not see nor ever know. I felt dizzy. At times, the forest in all its wild vitality itself appeared alive as a single entity, as if its untold variety of living creatures had merged into a unified life form. Rainwater filtered down through each layer of the canopy on its slow descent to the forest floor, falling long after it had ceased to fall from the clouds. Then it rose as steam and returned to the sky. The forest exhaled.

This was a National Forest, one of the patchwork of categories that locks islands of rainforest away in Brazil and protects them from development and deforestation. As such, the 5440-square-kilometre Tapajós forest felt reassuring.

But this forest was less something to celebrate than a reminder of what happens when you build roads into the forest. Human settlements and the region's growing soybean footprint surrounded the Floresta Nacional do Tapajós on three sides. Getting here in a car took just 30 minutes from downtown Santarém, provided you didn't get stuck in traffic. Yes, it was a magical place. But it was so isolated that it felt like a botanical garden masquerading as genuine forest.

Deeper into the Amazon, where Chris Clark lived, far larger swathes of intact forest survived, pristine and untroubled. To reach them I would have to travel beyond where the paved road ended.

# 3

# Manaus

*2018*

On the morning flight from Santarém, Manaus, any city, seemed unlikely. The forest unfurled in an unbroken carpet of green to the far horizon. Nose pressed against the plane's window, beset with the romantic notion that I might see an indigenous settlement with a foothold in the forest, I searched for a clearing, for a plume of smoke from a cooking fire, for any human outpost. I saw nothing. From time to time, a narrow river cut a lonely path through the monotony. An occasional raptor circled far below, a tiny speck against the horizontal wall of green. Were our plane to fall from the sky, the forest was so dense and the canopy so deep that we would most likely disappear without a trace. Like an ocean, the forest would swallow our plane, leaving barely a scar upon the surface.

Storm fronts worthy of an apocalypse gathered in the distance. Great cloud towers, kilometres high, billowed and turned the forest dark. Nearer by, storm clouds moved and re-formed, in constant motion, like a time-lapse film sped up for dramatic effect. It was raining away to the north. Otherwise, the sky was mute and the scale was terrifying. Bleached of colour to the dullest of greens by the relentless sun, so vast as to encompass countless weather zones, the Amazon here felt somehow eternal. This was an old place. And yet, not far from here, the forest was already gone.

Seen from the air, Manaus broke any spell of wilderness. The forest thinned to reveal tin-roofed slums strangling the city fringe and eating away at the forest. Wild nature was in permanent surrender, everywhere in retreat. In more affluent neighbourhoods, white apartment towers rose above mani- cured stands of garden. It was a poor person's Rio de Janeiro, a faux riverine Miami. A messy flotilla of pleasure craft, fishing vessels and cargo ships crowded the waterfront, and the three and a half kilometres of the Ponte Rio Negro, the first bridge to span the Amazon or any of its major tributaries, shone white in the late-morning sun.

The plane banked sharply. Forest filled the window. For a terrifying moment, I lost all perspective, convinced that we were plunging towards the Earth.

Manaus is a city of the Rio Negro, and it sprawls down to where the dark-watered Negro meets the lighter Solimões. The forests are not the only thing to have gone from here. Gone, too, is the story of those who lived here before there was a city.

*Manaós* means 'mother of the gods' and was the name of the indigenous people who once inhabited the area. Having given their name to the city, they disappeared and were never heard from again.

Portuguese settlers founded Manaus in 1669, but it was no Belém. It had many names. One was the 'Fort of São José on the Rio Negro'. Others called it the 'City on the Banks of the Black River'. It began as a frontier military garrison with one eye on ambitious Dutch colonies to the north and the rapacious Spanish Empire to the west. For most of its history, Manaus simply clung to the riverbank, a desolate place on the outer reaches of empire. Even as late as 1867, a German visitor wrote that Manaus was 'an insignificant little town of about three thousand inhabitants, with unpaved and badly levelled streets, and low houses and cottages of the most primitive construction without any attempt at architectural beauty'.

Long before this, from the earliest days of the colonies, the Amazon and its plant life had been endlessly fascinating to outsiders, and Manaus was where they began their expeditions. Botanists disappeared from here into the forest. Months, sometimes years later, they emerged, kilograms lighter, a faraway look in their eyes, and weighed down with plant specimens previously unknown to science. One expedition to the western Amazon in the 1820s returned to Europe with 6500 different species.

None of this was, of course, new to the Amazon's indigenous peoples, who already had an encyclopaedic knowledge of their natural environment. North of the Rio Negro, the Waimiri-Atroari used hundreds of different plant species from the surrounding forest in all aspects of their daily lives. They used one plant to treat fever. Another was perfect for crafting canoes. Yet another played a special role on ceremonial occasions. Some just tasted good. In one hectare (10,000 square metres) of forest close to a Waimiri-Atroari village, the Indians named and used 214 different plants. There and elsewhere, local fishermen added the sap from a liana known as *timbó* to a small stream, then sat back and waited. In no time, unconscious fish floated to the surface as locals filled baskets and sang songs to the forest's great abundance.

For all the excitement over the Amazon's abundant plant life, nothing intrigued European visitors quite like *caoutchouc*, or natural rubber, a curiously elastic form of latex which grew at low densities across the Amazon.

Every valuable natural resource to transform the world has its mother lodes. These are the places, mythic or real, whose names resonate through history with the reflected glow of untold riches, and of lives and societies forever transformed. For gold it is California and Australia's Victorian goldfields, El Dorado and the mines of King Solomon. Oil has the Arabian Peninsula and Texas. For rubber, it will always be Manaus.

The Aztecs and the Maya had used rubber for waterproofing and for making containers. It took a while to catch on, because early European explorers to the Amazon had eyes only for gold. The search for El Dorado and its gold blinded the Spaniards in particular, and it would take centuries before rubber reached Europe. In 1745, Frenchman Charles Marie de La Condamine, whom we have already met in Belém, presented this strange substance to a rapt audience at the Académie Royale des

Sciences in Paris. Even then, it took Europe's scientists nearly a century to unlock its potential. In 1839, self-taught chemist Charles Goodyear stumbled upon the process of vulcanisation, combining rubber with sulphur over a hot flame to create the flexible, pliable material we know today. Manaus was perfectly placed for what came next.

The rubber boom in Manaus was a strange affair, not least because Henry Wickham's act of agricultural grand larceny at Santarém in 1876 had doomed it even before it began. In 1880, when no one yet knew the extent nor understood the consequences of Wickham's treachery, Brazil exported 7000 tons of rubber from its river ports. By 1887, that figure had risen to 17,000 tons. A decade later, rubber exports reached 34,500 tons.

Blessed with a deepwater port in the heart of the most lucrative rubber terrain on earth, Manaus was quickly transformed. 'In London and New York,' wrote Wade Davis, 'men and women flipped coins to decide whether to go after gold in the Klondike or black gold in Brazil.' Soon, 5000 fortune seekers were arriving in Manaus every week on overcrowded riverboats. On arrival, most headed out directly to stake their claims in the surrounding forest. When the boom began in earnest in 1884, just a few thousand people lived here. By 1890, the population reached 10,000. By 1900, Manaus had 50,000 people.

Local landowners and traders could scarcely believe their good fortune. One minute they were rough-cut provincials looked down upon by the rest of Brazil as uncouth dilettantes at the table of the country's emerging, if fragile, prosperity. The next, fawning dignitaries, socialites and petty officials rushed to Manaus with unseemly haste.

The transformation of Manaus was an astonishing thing. The rubber barons made fast fortunes, and conspicuous consumption became a sport among them. As historian Robin Furneaux noted, 'If one rubber baron bought a vast yacht, another would install a tame lion in his villa, and a third would water his horse on champagne.' The wealthy of Manaus sent their laundry to Lisbon and to Paris. At home, the barons lit their cigars using US$100 banknotes. Brothels were everywhere, and the most sought-after courtesans attracted fees of US$8000 a night. 'Guests once knelt to lap champagne from the bathtub of the naked beauty Sarah Lubousk from Trieste,' wrote Furneaux. For a time, the people of Manaus were the world's highest per-capita consumers of diamonds.

These extravagances were mere foreplay, an aperitif at the lavish banquet that the authorities in Manaus had planned. In 1893, ambitious young colonel Eduardo Gonçalves Ribeiro became the governor of the Brazilian state of Amazonas. He oversaw an almost unlimited budget. In 1897, Manaus was one of very few Brazilian cities to have electric street lighting. Three years later, the local authorities installed an electric tram system, at a time when Boston and New York relied on horse-drawn streetcars. Soon the city had Brazil's first phone system, and a university. There were hospitals, schools, a zoo and a public library. Gentleman's outfitters shared the streets with a bullring. British architects designed the Municipal Market in 1901, and Scottish engineers oversaw the construction of the city's floating port.

More than useful utilities and necessary infrastructure, however, Gonçalves Ribeiro wanted legacy projects. He wanted buildings that made a statement. Gonçalves Ribeiro understood that his ongoing popularity depended on how well he played to the Brazilian obsession with Europe. To this day, many wealthy Brazilians see Europe as the benchmark. They long to be in Europe, and when they must be in Brazil, they long to make their lives as European as they can. Writing of Brazil's literary and cultural milieu in 2003, Peter Robb observed: 'The point of reference was Paris. Fashionable Rio deferred to Paris in almost everything, making only the odd exception for the British when quality manufacture or efficiency of operation really mattered, as it did for gabardine and railways. Elegance in Rio—sartorial, gastronomic, intellectual—always aspired to be French and it still does.' In this, Manaus in the nineteenth century was a very Brazilian creation. Rubber offered the city the once-in-a-lifetime chance to escape its destiny, to throw off the chains of geography and hitch a ride to Europe. Gonçalves Ribeiro modelled his Palácio de Justiça on Versailles. But his pride and joy was the Teatro Amazonas.

As an opera house, the Teatro Amazonas had very little to do with the earth upon which it stood. The architects sourced the marble for their grand pillars and porticos from Carrara in Italy. Also from Italy came the Venetian glass for the chandeliers, the gold leaf from Florence, and the ball-room tapestries. The mirrors were from France, as were the Louis XV furnishings and the 66,000 elaborate ceramic tiles from Alsace-Lorraine. The ironwork came from Glasgow. Almost the only local influences, aside from the overarching aspiration to be European, were the impoverished labourers who put it all together. That, and a fantasy-fuelled painting of an Amazonian water nymph that adorned the 20-metre-high stage curtain. That curtain rose for the first time on 7 January 1897, when the great and good of Manaus society crowded into this gilded folly to see the Grand Italian Opera Company's opening performance of Amilcare Ponchielli's Italian opera *La Gioconda*. It was the nineteenth-century cultural equivalent of Muhammad Ali and George Foreman's 'Rumble in the Jungle'. When French geographer Auguste Plane announced that 'The most refined civilisation has reached the Rio Negro!' you could sense an entire country swelling with pride.

Gonçalves Ribeiro was unrepentant about the cost. 'I found a village and turned it into a modern city,' he noted triumphantly. 'When the growth of our city demands it, we'll pull down this opera house and build another.'

Such was the glitter surrounding Manaus that, for a time, it became known as the Paris of the Tropics, although the name owed more to local aspiration than any real equivalence. The city's patina of sophistication could not conceal the brutal truth that Manaus was more Marseilles than it ever was Paris. The city had far more hyperbole than class: the brothels that spilled over into every street; the gaudy appropriation of borrowed style; and the tawdry antics of its new-money high society, drunk on their sudden, fabulous wealth.

But Henry Wickham's betrayal soon took its toll. Brazil had more than 300 million wild rubber trees that were native to Amazonia, but they spread thinly over some five million square kilometres, which made them difficult to harvest. Of the 70,000 seeds Wickham sent from Santarém, barely 2400 germinated. But it was enough. As the trees in Britain's colonies matured, it became far easier to harvest commercial quantities of rubber from the concentrated monoculture plantations in British Asia than rely on far-flung Amazonian rubber-tappers. In 1913, less than a third of the world's rubber came from Malaya and Ceylon (Sri Lanka). Seven years later it was 60 per cent. The decline of Manaus was as swift as had been its rise. Fortunes were lost overnight. Banks foreclosed on epic levels of debt. The fickle hangers-on who clung to the purse strings of the wealthy sniffed the wind and fled the city in their thousands. An epidemic of suicide swept the city among those who remained. And the lights literally went out as the much-vaunted electrical grid collapsed into ruin. Only cut-price brothels remained. They could, after all, operate by lantern light.

Even the Teatro Amazonas turned out to be an illusion. It could seat barely 700 paying patrons. With such meagre takings at the box office, massive government subsidies kept the lights on. But who would pay for the finest European performers and their sets to cross the Atlantic and journey days upriver into the jungle? A large proportion of performers in one visiting troupe died of yellow fever. A dysentery outbreak ravaged another. *La Gioconda*—whose plot line ends with corpses floating in a city's canals and amid a ruin on a remote island—was the only major opera performed at the Teatro Amazonas. It closed its doors in 1920.

If ever a real-life metaphor were needed for the rise and stunning decline of Manaus, it came in the figure of Eduardo

Gonçalves Ribeiro. The governor's fall from grace was sudden and spectacular. His enemies removed him from power in 1900. Rumour has it that he died soon after as the victim of strangulation in a sexual orgy gone awry.

These days, Manaus is like any Brazilian city that has burst beyond its historic core and consumed the wilderness with slums and a Spoleto restaurant on every corner. It owes everything to the Amazon, to river and to forest. And yet its very existence is designed to destroy both. It is the ultimate frontier city that obliterated the frontier. Two million people now live in Manaus. The largest river on earth flows past the city, but half a million people here have no access to clean running water. In 2015, a drug turf war engulfed the city, as graphically described in Chris Feliciano Arnold's *The Third Bank of the River*. 'If the old Manaus was built on balls of rubber,' Arnold wrote, 'the new Manaus was built on bricks of coke.' Brazil is now a net importer of rubber.

Manaus remains a city in love with large infrastructure projects that open to great fanfare but that are not really needed. Once it was the Teatro Amazonas. Now it is the Arena da Amazônia. Built for the 2014 FIFA World Cup, the stadium's design evokes local basket-weaving traditions. It hosted four first-round matches, a handful of games at the 2016 Rio Olympics, a single international match between Brazil and Colombia in 2018, and a World Cup qualifier in 2021. Its 44,300-spectator capacity is well beyond the needs of the local football team, Manaus Futebol Clube, who play in the fourth tier of Brazil's football league. They play only their biggest games, of which there are few, at the Arena da Amazônia. More often, they avoid the embarrassment of empty seats by playing at the modest 10,400-capacity Estádio da Colina. Otherwise, the Arena da Amazônia lies empty, save for the occasional concert or evangelical Christian event. The stadium cost US$270 million (A$330 million) to build and is a beautiful, useless thing.

I didn't like Manaus at all. In the streets surrounding the Teatro Amazonas, with its salmon-coloured façade and shiny cupola, armed paramilitaries and riverboat touts outnumbered passing foot traffic by ten to one. Manaus was broken footpaths beneath high-rise towers of glass and concrete, stained with mould; young men lounged in the shadows. Manaus was samba and bossa nova and Tropicalismo and car horns and a sudden awareness of sewage; the fetid stench caught in the throat and I felt it in the pores of my skin in the heat and humidity of a tropical afternoon. In each flinch or furtive look over uniformed shoulders, with each siren sound or shouted conversation, there lurked a sense that things could very rapidly spiral out of control. River and forest felt very far away.

Before I left Manaus for the final leg of my journey to Chris Clark and Xixuaú, I rented a car and drove north along the BR-174. The BR-174 is one of the Amazon's most controversial roads, a reminder that Brazil's indigenous people rarely win when they stand in the path of progress.

As far back as 1847, cattle ranchers from the fertile savannahs of Brazil's far north had been demanding such a road. In

1922, city representatives from Boa Vista, capital of Roraima state, north of Manaus and the Amazon, petitioned then-president Epitácio Pessoa for a land link to Manaus. They described themselves as 'virtually exiled from our mother country, almost without direct contact with national life'. In 'this distant piece of Brazil lost beyond the Equator,' they pleaded, they were 'defenceless against the ambitions of foreign envy, without a telegraph, without a regular postal service, and without efficient means of communication'. Theirs was indeed one of Brazil's most isolated corners, accessible only by river or by air. By the late 1960s, the proposed 775-kilometre road from Manaus to Boa Vista and on to Venezuela was a cause célèbre among those who argued that the Amazon's forests were a barrier to national development and progress. Local politicians who pushed the project found ready support among military planners. In 1970, Brazil's military government finally relented.

The road sliced through the lands of the Waimiri-Atroari indigenous people. It began as a civilian construction project. But when the Waimiri-Atroari began attacking construction crews, more than 500 soldiers from the 6th BEC battalion of military civil engineers took over. Any Waimiri-Atroari man, woman or child caught out in the open was shot on sight. Soldiers even pursued the Waimiri-Atroari deep into their territory, far from any roads. Many miles up the Jauaperi River, there is a beach called the Playa do Vinte e Oito (the 'Beach of the 28'), where soldiers massacred 28 Waimiri-Atroari civilians.

As one survivor described it: 'Helicopters flew over the villages, spilling poison and detonating explosives over hundreds of Indians who were meeting to celebrate rites of passage. White men in uniform attacked those who survived with guns and knives, cutting their throats. Tractors destroyed plantations, trails and sacred places.'

The Waimiri-Atroari were famously known as one of Brazil's most warlike tribes. They had resisted invasion long after other indigenous nations had succumbed. Perhaps this is why the soldiers wrought such terrible violence upon them. What the soldiers began, epidemics brought by the road construction crews finished. As one Waimiri-Atroari man told investigators many years afterwards, 'Before this road we lived well and in peace. We were healthy. After the road, people died and we were threatened.' When construction of the BR-174 began, there were perhaps 3000 Waimiri-Atroari. When the highway opened in 1977, less than 400 remained.

The Brazilian authorities and their partners weren't finished with the Waimiri-Atroari. Soon after the road opened, the mining behemoth Paranapanema seized 526,000 hectares (5260 square kilometres) of Waimiri-Atroari land for a tin-ore mine. They did so on the false pretext that there had been 'no reported presence of Indians in the north-east part of the Waimiri-Atroari reserve'. Then, in 1985, construction began on the Balbina Dam, along the Uatumã River north-east of Manaus. To build the dam, the authorities and their commercial partners, Manaus Energia, excised nearly 3000 square kilometres of land from supposedly protected Waimiri-Atroari indigenous territory. And for what? The poorly designed dam has extremely shallow, stagnant waters and more than 150 islands. The rotting trees of the flooded forest have produced what one report described as an 'acid broth'. Balbina now sends more methane into the atmosphere than ten coal-fired power plants.

In 1997, the authorities paved the BR-174, causing more disruption and deforestation.

I drove out to the BR-174 through the ragged outskirts of Manaus, past housing estates and truck parks and squalid slums. The traffic was awful, and it took an hour to clear the city. At one point, a grimy man dressed in rags stood in the middle of the road, brandishing a wheel jack and glaring at the cars that swerved around him.

Close to Manaus, low-slung forest lined the roadside. It didn't last long. What remained was patchy and there was always a building of some kind within sight of the road. At Presidente Figueiredo, Sunday day-trippers from Manaus crowded dusty roads beneath tall trees that gave an illusion of forest. Here the Amazon was a plaything for bored city folk.

Increasingly, open land took over. Towns were few, but it didn't seem to matter, as the forest had long before disappeared from here anyway. Beyond the roadside shanties of Manoel João de Souza, I entered a dystopian world where the landscape smouldered in the aftermath of fire. The forest here existed only in the memory of old people and as burnt silhouettes against a bright sky. Thin cattle grazed atop poor soils tinged with green. Blackened tree stumps and soy plantations, and degraded dirt fields extended from the road as far as I could see. Dust clouds blew to the horizon. In the ten years after the road opened in 1977, the human population along the BR-174 doubled. It has only continued to grow in the decades since.

And then came an apparition, as abrupt as any I have encountered in a lifetime of standing where the natural world meets the world of people. Like a scene from *The Lord of the Rings*, a wall of impossibly tall trees ran east–west to the horizon, standing guard like some impregnable natural fortress. Here was the Terra Indígena Waimiri-Atroari. Created in 1989, covering a vast 2,585,910 hectares (25,859 square kilometres), this protected indigenous homeland is a refuge for the Waimiri-Atroari, and for the land they inhabit and revere. Like the manifestation of Waimiri-Atroari ancestors taking a defiant last stand against the world and its destructive ways, the trees put a stop to the madness all around.

Indigenous territories make up around a quarter of the Amazon. They cover 12 per cent of Brazilian territory. But less than 1 per cent of the Amazon's deforestation has occurred on land held by its indigenous custodians. It is an old adage among those who care about the Amazon: if you want to protect the forest, give it to the Indians. It is another story altogether on the lands that surround these protected indigenous areas. The scenes of devastation here on the cusp of the Terra Indígena Waimiri-Atroari are not unusual in the Amazon.

The forerunner of all of South America's protected indigenous areas was the Xingu Indigenous Park, created in 1961. 'By 2010,' writes John Hemming in *People of the Rainforest*, 'half the land of the upper Xingu basin immediately around the park had been totally deforested—some 60,000 sq km (23,000 sq miles), which is more than twice the size of the park itself. This uncontrolled destruction locks the Indians' homeland in a lethal embrace. Everyone who flies into the Xingu is struck by the stark boundary between its green luxuriance and the brown waste outside.'

My journey ended at a checkpoint where the BR-174 entered the forest. Beyond the boom gate, the road continued into the Waimiri-Atroari lands, where the forest remained gloriously intact. Some 120 kilometres to the north, the road re-emerged. There, where Waimiri-Atroari land ended and the modern state of Roraima took over, the denuded landscapes returned.

Every night, boom gates guarded by the Waimiri-Atroari come down at either end of the highway, and only a small number of commercial buses and emergency vehicles may continue through the forest after dark. To protect the wildlife and wild people who inhabit the forest, no private vehicles may enter until first light, when the checkpoints open again. Cheap hotels, juice stands and steaming cauldrons of street food minister to those who must wait out the night here.

The checkpoint—the very idea of it—was a thing of wonder, as impressive as the wall of trees. As far as I am aware, this is the only national highway on Earth to be closed in this way on the orders of a land's indigenous people.

Uplifted, I turned the car around and returned down the road through the wastelands, smiling all the way back to Manaus.

# 4

# To Xixuaú

*2018*

Only too happy to leave Manaus, we sped south across the bridge in the gathering gloom of evening. Gilberto, my driver, was a man of few words and none were in English, which, I suppose, mattered little because he had the radio turned to full volume for much of the way. He took a while to get going, but once we were free of the Manaus traffic, he gained speed in inverse proportion to the light as he propelled us north-west along the south bank of the Rio Negro. I clung to the dashboard, fearing for my life. Even so, I was weary of planes and cars and cities, and I just wanted to arrive.

All paved roads end in Novo Airão where, I hoped, Christopher Clark would be waiting for me. Communications had been difficult, as they often are in the Amazon, and I was not entirely sure that Clark had made it downriver to meet me, nor when we would leave for the north. All going well, we would travel together by river up the Rio Negro tomorrow, then north along the Jauaperi, all the way to Xixuaú. The plan had been weeks in the making. I hoped it would happen.

At first, close to Manaus, the Rio Negro had flickered into view beyond the trees. Then the tropical darkness fell like a curtain as we hurtled into the night. The weather held just long enough for us to arrive in Novo Airão. One minute, I was counting stars through the car's open window. Children played in the main square. People lounged on plastic chairs outside the bars. Then came the rain with a sudden intensity that happens only in the tropics. Water came down in sheets, filling potholes and cascading down through the yellow glow of streetlights. Everybody ran for cover. Gilberto, suddenly subdued, inched the car through the deserted streets.

The downpour ended as suddenly as it had begun, and Gilberto took me to see Clark at his home. There he stood, shirtless, with long, lank hair and cheap thick-rimmed glasses that magnified his eyes. In a thick Glaswegian accent that nearly 30 years in Brazil had done little to soften, Clark was polite. But our conversation was halting and brief as we made the small talk that, I would later learn as I got to know him, Clark hated as much as I did. And, anyway, both Clark and I knew that the real conversations between us would not take place until we were alone and out on the river, far from here. There were other people around, but he didn't introduce us. Aside from Gilberto, whom I barely knew, I couldn't make out their faces in the dark. Clark had everything under control, and we made plans to leave early the next morning.

~

The day dawned pink out over the Rio Negro. Ungainly iguanas clambered through the branches overhanging the water, looking for food scraps from the Pousada Bela Vista, a small riverside guesthouse where I slept, while a few small fishing boats hurried back and forth along the river down below. On the far shore, an unbroken line of forest began at the water's edge and continued as far as I could see. For the first time since I arrived in Brazil, I felt as if I were in the Amazon.

In the early morning, at the base of a near-vertical wooden staircase that descended through the forest to the riverbank, Clark waited for me in a small aluminium boat. The boat had room for Clark, me, my backpack, and the supplies of food and fuel that we would carry upriver, little else. We stopped briefly at a floating petrol station. Clark already seemed more at ease than he had been the night before. Not long after my visit, a TV production team from Britain's Channel 5 were due to arrive. Clark spoke of how he hoped that he would be able to deflect the focus of the filming away from him and onto Xixuaú and his work there. Presented by Ben Fogle, the show would be an episode in the series *New Lives in the Wild*. Clark had done plenty of media work in his time. He wasn't hopeful.

If Woody Allen were a conservationist, he would look something like Chris Clark. Utterly unconcerned with appearances, he was both cerebral and devoid of pretension. He was scathing and humorous in turn. And he was impatient with incompetence. A couple of times, I threatened to upend us into the river, and he eyed me suspiciously as I moved awkwardly around the boat. I knew that he had not yet decided whether to tell me his story. He told me that he would make that decision when he was ready. I had limited time, but I knew that I had to wait. It was better to allow our relationship to evolve, even if it did so at the pace of the Rio Negro, which moved past, sluggish as a sloth. We eased out onto the river. The boat pushed hard against the current.

~

There are three kinds of river in the Amazon.

One of these I had already seen at Santarém. The Tapajós is what's known as a clearwater river. From the south, rivers such as the Tapajós and the Xingu, the Tocantins and the Araguaia, feed the main branch of the Amazon. From the north comes the Rio Trombetas. All of these clearwater rivers (except the Rio Trombetas) drain the Brazilian Shield, which is, according to John Hemming, 'one of the most ancient geological forma-tions on Earth'. Because they carry no silt, he writes, 'these streams are almost as pure as distilled water. They are not black from leaf litter tannin because their headwaters are in savannahs, and the absence of sediment is because their beds are flanked by broad sandy beaches and stable banks. These beautiful rivers reflect the deep blue of the sky and in the dry season are framed by creamy, rippled sand banks.'

So-called whitewater rivers, on the other hand, rise in the Andes, a mountain range far younger and far less stable than the Brazilian Shield. Rivers of western Amazonia—the Madeira, the Japurá and the Jutaí among them—carry with them the sediments, salts and solids that erode inexorably off the Andes, and they come together to form the Solimões, the

41

main branch of the Amazon. These rivers are milky-brown, a colour that ultimately wins out over more transparent rivers that join them on their way to the sea. Mosquitoes plague their waters.

The Rio Negro, which would be the world's second-largest river were it not part of the Amazon River basin, is a blackwater river. It is a very different river, less fertile than others that drain the Brazilian interior, though no less old. Blackwater rivers such as the Negro rise in the continent's north, in the Guiana Shield of Venezuela, Guyana, Colombia and northern Brazil. At their source, the rocks from which they emerge may be 500 million years old; these rocks ceased to erode long before the Amazon was even a river. The Rio Negro and its tributaries flow over the Guiana Shield's Precambrian sandstone without taking any trace with them on their currents. The dark colour comes not from sediments but from the forests through which they pass: falling leaves and rotting vegetation stain the water with humic acid, and the dark waters here have what Wade Davis has described as 'a tannin-content equal to that of a well-brewed cup of tea'.

Settlements here on the Rio Negro were few. Even so, as we travelled north-west upriver, we had not yet left the outside world behind. Two- and three-tiered riverboats, the work-horses of the Amazon, chugged to and fro, and an occasional ferry passed us by. In all this activity, there remained an aware-ness of Novo Airão and its satellites. An occasional house kept watch over the riverbank. Boats rested in the shallows while white-shirted workers scurried on deck to prepare meals for tourists on their return from forays into the forest's edge.

The dark waters flowed through channels that snaked between sandbanks, and Chris Clark knew them all. This was a time of flood along the Rio Negro, the season when the rivers of the Amazon come down from their watersheds to inundate riverine forests. Here amid the archipelago of islands and narrow *igarapés* (creeks), it was difficult for me to know where the river ended and where dry land began. From a distance, it seemed clear. But up close, most trees had their feet deep in water, and the river flood submerged the forest well beyond what I had imagined to be the riverbank. How far it went was impossible to see, so dark was the water and so tangled were the branches below the surface. The river had invaded and taken over the forest. Land was no longer land. At times we entered the flooded forest. At others, sand islands lay just beneath the surface over which we travelled.

The settlements thinned. Other boats were few. We had crossed a threshold, although there was nothing obvious to mark the moment. Like any journey across an invisible frontier—entering the Sahara or the Australian outback, for example, or the open ocean—the realisation comes suddenly after the boundary has been crossed: you know it when you see it. In the desert it comes to me in the moment when I can hear the wind, when nothing else exists to drown out the gusts. On an ocean, it is the absence of shorebirds. The moment on the river came when I realised that there were no other boats, and nor had there been for some time. Nor were there any houses or settlements, even on the far shore, which I could just make out away to the south. Forest crowded the riverbank, dense, dark and implacable. I stole a glance at Clark behind me to see if he had noticed it too, but his face was a mask. This was a journey he had made many times before, and his frontier was doubtless different to mine. We left behind the Rio Negro and turned up the Jauaperi, taking a narrow channel called the Paraná do Cantagalo.

I had gone beyond such a frontier of the mind many times in a lifetime of adventures, although, unlike Clark, I have never made such a place my home. Every time, I had felt fear and exhilaration in equal measure. But it was easier when I was younger, when I had no children, when my parents were healthy. Not since I had crossed the Kalahari Desert in Botswana two years before had I gone so thoroughly off grid as I was doing now in my quest for Xixuaú. For the next ten days, perhaps two weeks, I would have no clear means of contacting the outside world, nor could the outside world reach me. The phone in the village of Xixuaú, across the lagoon from Clark's home where I would be staying, *might* function. They had been having problems with the satellite dish in recent weeks and there were no guarantees. Should something happen, no one could reach me. I felt no sense of foreboding. But I remained haunted by a time when the unthinkable nearly happened.

In August 2015, with my father in hospital, I decided that he was well enough for me to hurry to Madagascar on an assignment. He was in a rehabilitation hospital, receiving treatment for the cancer that had stalked him for a decade. He had always refused to become downcast. Even in the hospital, unable to walk and with no prospect of ever returning home with the use of his legs, he was reconciled, even hopeful of a few more years. A man of faith, he didn't so much believe in the power of positive thinking as embrace it, unable to live any other way.

He had always been the faithful follower of my journeys, taking vicarious pleasure in the places I'd seen and the people I had met. Whether in the Kalahari or here in the Amazon or out the back of Bourke, I thought often of my father, and wondered what he would make of each place. His relationship with nature had always been distant but affirming—he believed in it and would speak often and warmly on its behalf. But he would never have taken the risks I often did. His experience of nature was remote. He had never travelled to Africa or South America, never heard a lion roar nor stared into the forest hoping to see a jaguar. To him, nature was God's creation, and if he never saw nor heard a lion and never put himself in selfish danger, or if he never went to the wild places of the planet, well, that was undoubtedly God's plan, and who was he to wonder why?

Before I left the hospital on my way to the airport and on to Madagascar, we spoke of the future, of seeing each other upon my return. We talked of lemurs and baobab forests and of what life might hold for him now that he would never walk again. When I exited his room and walked away down the hospital corridor, I stopped in mid-step, suddenly convinced that I had left something unsaid. If it was a premonition, I didn't understand it at the time. I stood, gripped by the impulse, but not knowing what it was that I should say. I walked quietly back to the door of his room. He had turned his face to the wall, and his lips moved silently in prayer. He didn't see me and, not wanting to interrupt a moment of such intimacy, I walked away, badly shaken.

Two weeks later, perhaps a little more, I emerged from Madagascar's Kirindy Forest where I had been looking for night lemurs and fossas and owls. For days I had been unable to raise a phone signal that might connect me with the outside world. As we rejoined the main road, a kestrel flew up and perched on a post by the roadside. It occurred to me that these were powerlines and that perhaps there was a mobile phone reception tower nearby. As one came into view, messages flooded in from Marina, my wife: my father had turned the sudden, final corner towards death. Crouched by a roadside puddle where women washed clothes, close to a remote Madagascan village whose name I never learned, I called him at the hospital. It was our final conversation.

Across the night roads of western Madagascar I raced, oblivious to danger and to any real sense of where I was. Somehow, days later, I made it home. Not long after I arrived at the hospital, at a moment when we were alone, there seemed to be a stirring of some kind behind his eyes, and I asked if he knew that I was there. 'This is Anthony, Dad. Can you hear me?' And with that, there was the merest flicker of light, the last that I would ever see in the eyes of my father. With a supreme effort, the last perhaps of his long life, he reached over and took my hand. What darkness did he know at that moment? Or was it light? And then he was gone.

Life, such as it was, remained with him. Great, deep, unearthly breaths racked his body, part of some great drama on the cusp between life and death. The light had gone, although his eyes remained half-open. The man who had been my father—a good, kindly, simple man—hung on for two days and two nights as I slept by his bedside, leaving only to eat. Gaps began appearing between his breaths. Then those gaps became longer. And precisely 40 years to the day since my grandfather had collapsed and died from a heart attack in front of five-year-old me, my father's heart stopped beating and he turned white as blood drained from his face. There was one more breath, an echo, the body's last reflex. And it was over. His life was over.

People talk of time standing still in moments such as these. But it was my world—my family's world—alone that stood still. Time marched on, and the rest of the world with it, yet for us, life would never be the same again. It was the end of innocence. All I remember is loss, unutterable loss, and a sudden sense of absence where once there had been life.

Three years later, I felt suddenly unmoored. I travel to remote corners of the Earth, to heal in places of silence, to places where I can listen to and make sense of the world, to places where I can mourn and rejoice. But I am forever frightened of what might happen while I am away. Now, here in the Amazon, on the Jauaperi river beyond the Rio Negro, I wished that my father had known this place. Even if that were not possible, I knew that he would have enjoyed hearing about this journey. On the Jauaperi, I wept quietly.

Forest and river. River and forest. The further we travelled up the Jauaperi, the more elemental the world became. An occasional riverboat flying a limp Brazilian flag. A small village or two dwarfed by trees. A distant vapour trail in the southern sky. These were the only signs that the forest didn't extend all the way to the end of the Earth, and that there might be a world beyond. Otherwise, there was only forest and river and a relentless sun. In places, the trees were so tangled that the forest felt like a single entity. So still was the water that trees and sky reflected perfectly in the dark Jauaperi waters; I lost count of the number of times that all perspective shimmered away and I had to look to the sky lest I lose my balance and tumble out of the boat.

At Gaspar—little more than chickens and dogs and a hut on stilts on a minor tributary off Jauaperi's east bank—we stopped to pick up Valdemar, who was to be my guide. A Baniwa Indian of uncertain age, Valdemar gathered up a few belongings and joined us in the boat. Clark introduced him as 'one of my oldest friends here'. I was filled with questions, but Clark was eager that we arrive at Xixuaú before nightfall.

'Valdemar's story is at the heart of the story here,' said Clark, sensing my impatience. 'There'll be plenty of time for that.'

A little further upriver, we passed São Pedro, a small village on the east bank of the river. 'This is where, in some ways, the story began,' he shouted over the noise of the outboard, before waving off my questions.

Further on again, smoke rose from the riverbank. Charred fields with blackened tree stumps stretched to the horizon where once there had been forest. Moments earlier, exuberant forest had surrounded us and this sudden desolation was dispiriting. It felt like a tableau for the modern Amazon, a triptych of a doomed land flanked on either side by pristine forest.

Clark and Valdemar surveyed the scene, their faces grim, exchanging knowing glances. It felt like the last days. Clark did not wait for me to ask. 'I'll tell you, too, about fire,' he said. *What did you expect?* he seemed to be saying. *Did you really think the Amazon would reveal its secrets on the first day?*

I sat back and resolved to wait.

On and on we travelled, further upriver and deeper through a forest whose inner reaches hid in stygian darkness. We sped past the wall of trees—unchanging yet never the same, mono-chrome green and yet a million shades of green—until it all became a blur. As sunset neared, great banks of clouds reflected in the river. They looked like monsters guarding the gates of the River Styx. Rain threatened but never arrived. Egrets and terns wheeled and dived. A sudden wind swept down the river. And still we travelled through it all, forging north through a world that was rare and remote and staggeringly beautiful.

Just when I wondered if this river might go on forever, we diverted from the east bank. Racing an approaching rain-storm, we made for a narrow gash in the trees on the west bank where a small river emerged from the forest and emptied into the Jauaperi. It looked no different from countless others we had passed.

We plunged into this narrow *igarapé* that twisted and turned, doubling back on itself before emerging into a broad lagoon, a lost world hidden from the Jauaperi by walls of forest. A small village lay away to our right. Two wooden houses on stilts rose above the floodwaters in a cleft of forest on our left. And everywhere all around, forest. The lagoon's waters were pink, catching the last moments of the day's sun. *Aras* (macaws) screeched like arrows across the sky. Giant *samaúma* trees rose above the forest to the north-west. A toucan came to rest on the uppermost branch of another *samaúma* across the lagoon. Closer at hand, a squirrel monkey watched us as it ate, just above eye level. A small pod of *boto*, the pink river dolphins of the Amazon, breached the water in perfect, playful arcs.

I was smiling so much my jaw ached. For the first time since I had met him, Clark's smile carried pure and unguarded joy.

Someone chopped wood in the village and an angry voice cried out. From somewhere, the mournful moan of howler monkeys pulsed through the forest in waves, impossible to place, echoing as if from the very gates of hell. Night fell like a curtain.

'That's right,' Clark said. 'Yes, that's right. Welcome to the Xixuaú.'

# 5

# Abundance

*2018*

Christopher Clark lived so deep in the forest that I wondered whether he might not be Robinson Crusoe in disguise. The journey here had been an epic of wonder and discovery. Arrival felt like crossing some threshold of absurd abundance, as if here was the Earth's cornucopia. In a single day, we had shed the skin of so-called civilisation and entered into the world of the primeval forest where nature held sway.

Forest surrounded on three sides the simple four-roomed hut that Clark shared with his family. It faced out onto the lagoon and had green, wooden plank walls, a roof of corrugated metal sheets, and windows without glass. The house rose on stilts above the floodwaters. A raised walkway extended out the back to a small toilet. Across the water were equally simple guest quarters where, in a concession to the sensibilities of visitors, potted flowers lined the walkway that connected the bedroom to the toilet.

We pulled up to the floating balsa platform that is standard in huts all across the Amazon, and climbed the wooden stairs. Clark introduced me to Artemizia, his wife. Artemizia was a pretty young Baniwa woman, who also happened to be Valdemar's daughter. Clark and Artemizia's eight-year-old daughter, Shenaya, was there, as were Raí, Artemizia's son from a previous relationship, and several of Valdemar's adult sons. It was a warm and unassuming place. If the surroundings were akin to paradise, then home was a hearth of close family bonds.

On that first evening, Clark and I sat on his narrow deck, which had room for little more than a ramshackle wooden table and two chairs. For the most part we sat in silence, and the silence here was like a spell. Valdemar later took me out in a wooden canoe to explore the lagoon. The only sound was wood on water, water on wood, as Valdemar dipped his paddle in the river that lapped against the side of the canoe. Stars were few. We heard rain drumming across the lagoon only seconds before it soaked us to the skin and drove us back to Clark's hut. After a meal of piranha and a caipirinha nightcap, I paddled a canoe across to my quarters where I lay awake until long after midnight, listening to the night sounds of the forest.

The rhythm in those early days at Xixuaú was that of the rainforest. We rose with the sun, waited out rainstorms in silence, and paddled through the flooded forest with no dry land anywhere to be found. Spider monkeys and tamarins, even the occasional howler monkey far from its troupe, watched our approach, ate warily, then crashed off into the undergrowth, screeching in alarm. Valdemar's sharp eye fixed on a sloth, high in the branches. Unable to outrun anything, living in a world where predators climb trees, the sloth has transformed inactivity into a virtue. Its grey-brown coat, too, is an ingenious and unlikely asset: each sloth hair contains tiny fissures or grooves that fill with algae and lichen and turn the sloth the green of the forest. Only the keenest senses will ever detect it. Almost imperceptibly, it turned to regard us from what Peter Matthiessen once described as 'an earless face like a husked coconut'.

Out on the open water, peace had reigned, but paddling into the flooded forest demanded careful attention as Valdemar cut a patient path through the branches that blocked our way. Valdemar and I shared no language, yet he was an attentive guide, cautious with flicking branches and barbed lianas. He was less careful with cobwebs, and I will forever shudder at the memory of passing through an unseen web where a spider, no doubt as surprised as I, attached itself to me. It covered my face—all of my face—for lifetime-long seconds. In the instant before I flinched and flicked frantically at my face, I saw the world through the sinuous legs of a gigantic spider. It was a jungle nightmare come true.

'*Tranquilo*,' Valdemar urged softly.

The flooded forest seemed to go on forever, but Valdemar somehow found dry land, and we walked along an enchanted trail. Armed with a machete, he pointed out to me the tracks of a herd of peccary (sometimes called the skunk pig), named the birds for me in Portuguese, and peeled back the leaf litter to show me the week-old scraping left by a jaguar. Knowing that a jaguar had passed this way, I stared intently into the forest, struck by the magic of it all. He pointed out spiders on gossamer threads so transparent that I wondered whether I had seen them at all. There were trees that could cure malaria, lilac orchids, and fungi that climbed tree trunks like ladders to some elven hideaway. And whenever I stopped to listen, Valdemar paused discreetly, waiting with the patience of the forest peoples.

Back on the boat, the canoe seemed like an extension of Valdemar's body, so calmly did he move and so obedient was it to his commands. Like so many indigenous people, Valdemar bore in every movement a certain wisdom—the only word I can find to describe it. In every machete flick, every slow paddle stroke, there was an economy of style and an air of quiet authority.

Down one *igarapé*, Valdemar faced the nose of the canoe into the forest. He listened, then twisted the paddle into the water, this way and that. As he did so, he unleashed a nasal call that to my untrained ear resembled both war cry and ritual incantation, but which turned out to be a convincing imitation of an animal in distress. In no time at all, an agitated family group of giant river otters surrounded us. These charismatic creatures, some 1.5 metres long, preened and bristled, lifting themselves half out of the water the better to get a look at us, squealing in indignation. Coming at us in a frenzy of mock charges and with the persistence of a street gang mobbing our canoe, they ducked and weaved and squalled. It was all terribly exciting, and not a little intimidating. Valdemar, of course, remained calm.

I spent many hours in this way, paddling with Valdemar the skein of waterways in search of wisdom and of wildlife, looking for jaguars and monkeys and macaws. We fished for *pirarucú*, a vast fish that has lungs and that weary fisherman kill by drowning. One late afternoon, in golden light, Valdemar took me back out beyond the lagoon and across the Jauaperi, which I had not seen since our arrival a few days before. In the canoe, we sat so low in the water that our legs were below the waterline. We cut diagonally across the Jauaperi's strong current and the current carried us downriver. Upon reaching the Jauaperi's eastern bank, we paddled back to the north along the main river. Valdemar knew where he was going, and behind the wall of trees lay a magical world of miniature lakes and flooded forest glades that had been wholly invisible from the main river. The water here was like glass, reflecting sky and forest in a tableau that left me reeling.

High above, in a shaded stand of aninga arum trees that grow in gallery forests such as these, the prehistoric hoatzin squawked and huffed and puffed, looking down upon us in high dudgeon. The blue, red and chestnut–coloured hoatzin, this 'archaic burnished-bronze fowl of the river brush', has what one naturalist described as 'a spiky crest like a punk haircut'. Unusually, hoatzin young have claws on their wings. These strange appendages date back to the age of the dinosaurs, and they serve hoatzin chicks well in times of flood when they use them to clamber from the water and climb up the nearest branch after they fall from the nest.

On our way back across the Jauaperi, paddling hard into the wind, another sudden storm swept down upon us. There was no way we could outrun it, and lightning struck the river, sending up a plume of water barely 50 metres north of where we crossed.

We sat on Clark's terrace. Down below, Shenaya and Raí took turns to jump from an overhanging branch into the water. Artemizia and her father cleaned the day's catch on the pontoon.

It was quiet here, peaceful, and none of us spoke unless we had to.

'There go the dolphins,' said Clark to no one in particular.

We turned slowly to follow them as they breached and dived, breached and dived.

Howler monkeys began their unearthly chorus that rippled through the forest.

'It's cold.' It was Clark again who spoke. 'By local standards, it's cold today.'

Valdemar agreed with a nod.

It rained for a while, stopped, then started up again in intense bursts. Rain drummed down on the water, a sound like an approaching freight train, then battered down on the tin roof before slowing again. Individual raindrops were the storm's last echo.

'It's unusual to have this much rain, so late in the season.'

When I didn't reply, after a pause, Clark repeated what he'd said, this time in Portuguese.

Valdemar grunted assent.

I had been waiting for Clark to tell me his story and the story of Xixuaú. But he was in no hurry and, I realised now, neither was I.

We got talking about the wildlife I had seen. Travellers in the Amazon are often disappointed with how few animals they see. I had been lucky: in my first few days, I had already seen dolphins and monkeys, giant otters and hoatzin and macaws and toucans. In this, Clark told me, Xixuaú was unusual. Although the Amazon is the most biodiverse place on the planet, seeing more than an unidentifiable concatenation of trees is more often a matter of chance. Unless you're exploring with the eye for detail of an entomologist holding a magnifying glass, the forest can seem like the natural world's best keeper of secrets.

Clark knew this all too well. He had been in the Amazon in some capacity for more than 30 years, and he had helped broadcasters from around the world—the BBC, CNN, and film crews from French, German and Italian television among them—film the region's wildlife.

'In the past, filmmakers approached us and told us what they wanted,' said Clark. 'I'd then inform all the locals at Xixuaú and we got to work. The guys went looking for the animals so that we had the animals in holding pens before the film crews arrived.'

Even jaguars?

'Even jaguars. We always asked them to film as quickly as possible so we could release them. We wouldn't do it now, and most broadcasters wouldn't want it known that the wild animals they filmed were in temporary captivity. But it's the only way they could do it. They're on tight time frames and budgets. They could never film the animals if it wasn't for the people who know where the animals are, and how to get them close enough to them to film them. Nobody could come from England or Germany or America and do that.'

Clark smiled at a memory.

'One time, we had a project with Canal 5 of France. They were doing underwater filming in Xixuaú for what was supposed to be a documentary about a nature reserve in Peru. But in the real location, the water was too dark for filming, so they came to Xixuaú. In advance of their filming, we netted an area of creek in the Xixuaú, and put in lots of fish, turtle species, caimans and an anaconda. We'd done all of this before. It was no big deal. Unbeknown to us, during filming an enormous caiman entered the enclosure by itself and the anaconda swam over it. The cameraman who was filming the snake got quite a fright when the caiman suddenly appeared and ate the anaconda. He did get some great footage, though.'

Clark poured me another caipirinha, warming to his theme.

'Some years back, a couple of marine biologists came here on holiday. They loved the place. Isabella, this professor from Naples University, said to me one day, "Chris, let's do a little experiment." And she had a little funnel net and a large glass jar. She attached the bottom rim of the net to this glass jar, and she said to me, "Go out into the river and row around for twenty minutes with this net in the water beside the canoe." Actually, it was quite hard work because it got really heavy! As I rowed around, the net filtered stuff into the jar. She then took this jar, put in a liquid that she had, closed it, and took it back to Naples where they examined it in the laboratory. She found 48 species of zooplankton in that glass jar. Twenty-six of them were unknown to science.'

Xixuaú felt to me like paradise. Clark knew better. He knew that Xixuaú was the closest we could come to paradise in a world where people lived. But he told me about one place he knew where the pristine Amazon survived.

A day's journey north of Xixuaú, a small river—more an *igarapé*, really—known as the Xiparina enters the Jauaperi, coming down from the north-west. Taking the Xiparina, it is not long before the creek narrows and becomes overgrown because no one ever passes that way. There comes a point when you must abandon the speedboats and take to the canoes. Armed with axes and saws and machetes, you inch your way upriver, cutting trail for two or three days. It is arduous, backbreaking work. Your reward is Buritizal.

The name comes from the buriti palm—a tree that Clark described as 'an incredibly beautiful palm tree with bunches of big red fruits'—that proliferates there like nowhere else in the Amazon. It is, in Clark's telling, truly a lost world of lakes filled with manatees, of palm groves that you can paddle through for an entire day, and where much of the wildlife has never before seen human beings.

Clark once travelled there with a producer from the BBC's Natural History Unit on a reconnaissance mission to scout future filming options. After making camp, they went for a swim. 'The water is really clear up there. You can put your fishing rod in the water and choose the fish that you want— that one's too small, that one's better, that one's better. And then turtles will come out of the undergrowth and come up to try and take the hook as well. Or you can be canoeing past and the turtles don't even drop off their logs. They're not even scared. Here, any time you go past a turtle, they're straight into the water. Up there, they're just sitting there looking at you as you go past. It's incredible—it's like Jurassic Park. Anyway, we dived off the aluminium boat we'd taken up. All of a sudden there's all this screaming and this huge group of giant otters comes into sight, charging towards us. Although you know that giant otters don't attack people, it is kind of scary if you're in the water and these big things are coming at you. There were like twelve of them or something. We were in the canoe *in a flash*, and we had to grab the producer and drag her into the canoe. She was so frightened. Even we got scared. It was quite amusing, actually.'

From May to July in Buritizal, hundreds, perhaps thousands of macaws nest high in the hollows of the palms. Clark told me that the macaws always give birth to two chicks. As the chicks grow feathers and become stronger, they move to the ledge—to wait for their parents to come and feed them, and to get a view of their surroundings. As Clark told it, 'They're getting closer and closer to being ready. Then one of the two *always* flies too soon. It takes off and—plop!—into the water. Once they're in the water, that's it.' Down below, caimans and anacondas lie in wait, growing fat on their annual diet of baby macaw. Clark remembered how after a day's filming they would paddle around and try to rescue as many floundering baby macaws as they could and restore them to their nests. 'Those things cost a fortune in pet shops around the world.'

On an expedition to Buritizal with a PBS film crew, Clark and Valdemar built a series of galvanised-steel platforms high in the palms. There, a cameraman would perch close to the macaw nests to film the birds as the parents came and went. Very early each morning, they took the cameraman to the site of his choice and then returned to camp to wait out the day.

On this occasion, they decided to go for a walk in the forest. They weren't expecting trouble and were armed only with machetes. (A machete is an essential piece of kit for anyone walking into an Amazonian forest. It is as useful for slashing a trail through the undergrowth as it is handy as a weapon of self-defence.) 'It is always an exciting feeling to set foot in a part of the Amazon that you know for sure nobody has set foot in before,' Clark would later write in his journal.

It was around 7 a.m., and the day was still cool. They had been walking for perhaps twenty minutes when Valdemar suddenly stopped and pointed. Barely 20 metres away stood a jaguar. It was side-on to the two men, but its head was turned towards them and was looking at them. It raised its tail, which began to swish back and forth in agitation. Valdemar had once hunted forest cats for their skins and knew what this meant.

'It's going to attack us,' Clark remembered him saying. Sure enough, the jaguar turned and walked slowly but deliberately in a direct line towards them. About halfway to them, the jaguar jumped up onto a fallen tree, stretched itself, and began sharpening its claws. They both knew that an attack was inevitable and that to run would be an act of suicide: the jaguar would bring one or both of them down within metres. In the forest, only food flees.

'Get ready!' Valdemar shouted. The two men stood shoulder to shoulder, clutching their machetes. Valdemar screamed at Clark, urging him to be steadfast and to not let go of his machete, no matter what. Still screaming, Valdemar implored Clark to hit the jaguar if it went first for Valdemar. He promised to do the same if the jaguar chose Clark. Clark just remembered screaming, somewhat less coherently. The jaguar came on at full speed, but shuddered to a halt, growling, barely a metre from the two men. Their machetes almost touched the jaguar's nose.

Clark remembered looking into the eyes of this jaguar. 'I could see this confusion, as if to say, "What am I getting myself into here?" I think it thought we were one animal. It probably had never seen human beings before: it thought it was going to get an easy meal. The fact that we didn't turn and run put doubt into its mind. And it made the right decision, because it could easily have hurt us, maybe even killed one of us, but we would have given it a couple of good whacks with the machete as well. For a solitary big cat, that would be a high price to pay. So it just stood there, looking at us. And there I was, just looking into the eyes of this cat.'

Time stopped. Years later, sitting on his deck in Xixuaú, Clark couldn't say how long they stood there. Perhaps it was all of twenty seconds. It felt like much longer. He became conscious of the sound of his own breathing, or at least he heard it when they weren't screaming. Their only hope lay in the cat's confusion. Human screaming was not something it had likely ever heard before. By hesitating, the jaguar had lost momentum. Clark remained convinced that this jaguar had no idea what the men were and that it had never seen a human being in its entire life.

'Then the jaguar *slooowly* turned and it *slooowly* started padding off,' Clark remembered. 'I took a couple of steps after it, and it went—*shung!*—off into the forest. Neither of us said a word.'

He sat back and smiled at the memory.

# 6

# Indian Country

*2018*

Valdemar was my constant companion whenever we left the hut at Xixuaú. His company was reassuring. When I was with him, we belonged in the forest. Otherwise, the world was a jungle. Like all indigenous people on their home terrain, Valdemar was at home here in ways that I never could be.

One afternoon, while we waited out a rainstorm nursing caipirinhas under a tin roof, I asked Clark and Valdemar about the Waimiri-Atroari. Their reserve borders Xixuaú to the north. At more than 2.5 million hectares (25,000 square kilometres), their territory is larger than the US states of Vermont, New Jersey or New Hampshire. In it live 1500, perhaps 2000 people.

In much of the Brazilian Amazon, indigenous and non-indigenous peoples rarely get on well. Here, it seemed, was no exception. 'Some of the older people on this river remember when there were bounties for killing an Indian,' said Clark. He gave the impression that not everyone thought that this was a bad thing. Even today, Clark told me, across the Amazon, *caboclos* (the mixed-race river people who form the backbone of riverbank communities), including some on the Jauaperi, whipped themselves into a frenzy of support whenever governments launched a campaign to teach the Indians a lesson.

Valdemar nodded in agreement.

'A lot of people here are totally against the Waimiri-Atroari,' Valdemar said to me. 'They don't like them. But thank God they are here, because if they weren't here in the area, everything would be finished. They are protecting a *massive* area that you could actually call a nursery for many species that then come downriver. And we have many more fish here than they have downriver, thanks to the fact that fish are coming out of the Indian areas. There are a lot of turtles in this river because the turtles can nest in peace up there. And on the rest of the river, it's almost impossible, except for now these isolated projects where they're trying to defend turtles. That's in general for all life, for all the animals and fish, almost everything.'

Clark agreed: 'The best protection of any land in the Amazon is under Indian control. If you really want it protected well, the Indians are best at it.'

Xixuaú once lay within the traditional lands used and inhabited by the Waimiri-Atroari. Xixuaú is an old Waimiri-Atroari name, although its meaning has been lost to time. Sadness flickers through such stories. I am a writer who believes in the transformative power of words, so I look upon the loss of such etymologies as one more step in the incremental poverty that defines our connection to the land and the diversity of life on our planet. This small, salient step walks us away from a time when we belonged to the land more than the land belonged to us. It is a chink in humankind's ancestral memory.

As David Campbell wrote in his beautiful memoir of the Amazon, *A Land of Ghosts*, 'there is a sure and necessary empowerment in naming things. Words—and numbers, too—may be weightless, as insubstantial as light, yet they are terribly powerful: they can start a war, order the strip-mining of a mountain, or trigger the secretion of endorphins. And names allow us to possess our environment and manipulate it in scaffolds of thought and design.' The loss of words and names in the Amazon, he wrote, 'destroyed the survivors' ability to understand their land and its diversity. Entire vocabularies disappeared.' Speaking of the name of the river Juruá from western Amazonia, Campbell wrote that, 'Like the names of most everything here, its meaning has gotten lost in the forgotten etymologies of vanished cultures; it has become a word without a context.'

And yet, if some salvation resides in the word Xixuaú, it does so in the new life breathed into this name and this place by Clark, Valdemar and their friends. Clark had lived here, on and off, for nearly three decades, and had championed its protection for almost as long. By doing so, by placing Xixuaú at the centre of his own life, perhaps he had revived its story and had given this place a meaning that somehow reconnects the thread that ties this place to its past.

I told Clark my theory as the rain eased. He looked at me but said nothing.

~

Historical references to the Waimiri-Atroari describe them as 'fierce' and 'warlike'. The real story is somewhat more complicated and is a classic frontier tale.

Indigenous peoples whose traditional homelands lay along the coast, or close to a major river or tributary, were all but wiped out by colonial armies and slaving expeditions from the sixteenth century onwards. In the seventeenth century, slaving expeditions carried out massacres and carried off indigenous slaves from the Rio Urubu on the margins of Waimiri-Atroari territory north-east of Manaus. Slaving and missionary posses first ventured up the Jauaperi in the eighteenth century. From their hideouts in their dense and remote forests, the Waimiri-Atroari watched the boats pass by along the Rio Negro and, from time to time, the Jauaperi. They knew what was coming. Until then, the absence of easily navigable rivers beyond the Jauaperi and the Rio Branco kept them hidden and, for the most part, protected. According to one report about the Waimiri-Atroari in early colonial times, 'When first contacted by the early spice hunters, their territory was one of the most feared and impenetrable in the Amazon.' By the middle of the nineteenth century, boats were not just passing by. Many stayed. Brazil became independent in 1822 and the new nation, hungry for land, began building settlements along the south bank of the Rio Negro.

The Waimiri-Atroari call themselves Kinja, or 'the people', and their land once stretched from deep in what is now Roraima all the way down to the north bank of the Rio Negro. As has always been the case on New World frontiers, the indigenous Waimiri-Atroari were seen as a barrier to progress, ranging across a vast swathe of land considered by the local and national authorities as both unproductive and ripe for exploration and exploitation. First came the soldiers, then the so-called *civilizados*—the settlers and traders who became the foot soldiers in Brazil's quest for land. As if a hostile and well-equipped force advancing on Waimiri-Atroari land was not provocation enough, the settlers and soldiers deliberately provoked the Indians. Armed traders lured the Waimiri-Atroari with promises of gifts, then carried them off in chains. Marcel Monnier, a French writer and traveller to the region at the time, wrote that the *civilizados* 'set fire to villages, led women and children off into captivity, and shot at the wretched men who tried to defend their huts against the invaders. From that day onwards the war was ignited and continued incessantly and implacably.'

The Waimiri-Atroari had little choice but to respond. In 1863, they launched a raid on Tauapeçaçu, close to where Novo Airão now stands. Two years later, they raided Airão, a south-bank Rio Negro town close to where the Jauaperi enters the Rio Negro from the north. In the same year, they attacked foreign boats on the Jauaperi itself. In 1873, they attacked other towns along the banks of the Rio Negro. Among them was Pedreira, and the population of Moura also fled before an advancing party of Waimiri-Atroari warriors. Emboldened, the Waimiri-Atroari were soon seizing most of the boats that travelled along the Rio Negro.

But it was the attacks on Pedreira and Moura that pushed the local authorities to abandon any restraint. Gunboats filled with soldiers and heavy weapons surged all the way up the Jauaperi. The Waimiri-Atroari were masters of their own rivers and forests: the soldiers captured nothing more than an empty canoe. One can imagine the soldiers in their frustration shooting incomprehensibly into the forest, like the French warship firing into a continent in *Heart of Darkness*.

The soldiers were able to turn the tide on what had become their own terrain, and then go after the Indians with new momentum. In late 1873, the military garrison at Moura pursued their Indian attackers after a raid and massacred hundreds of Waimiri-Atroari. The governor of Amazonas wanted an end to all this nonsense, and commissioned Lieutenant Antonio de Oliveira Horta to spend a year travelling up and down the Jauaperi, massacring any Indians he and his well-armed soldiers could find. By 1876, they had broken Waimiri-Atroari resistance. An unquiet peace followed, marked by skirmishes but little open conflict.

As ever in the Amazon, next came well-meaning missionaries and those seeking to 'make contact' with and 'pacify' indigenous peoples by non-military means. In 1881, the Waimiri-Atroari launched an attack on Moura and killed two settlers. Soon after, the renowned Brazilian naturalist João Barbosa Rodrigues ventured into the world of the Waimiri-Atroari. On the Jatapu River, Barbosa Rodrigues won over a suspicious Waimiri-Atroari war party with gifts of rum and machetes. In return, the Indians acceded to Barbosa Rodrigues's inexplicable suggestion that they settle on the Rio Negro. The Waimiri-Atroari never fulfilled their promise. It was just as well. The authorities in Manaus met Barbosa Rodrigues's plan with lip-curling dismay. Instead of sending more gifts, the governor sent a warship to fire on the Waimiri-Atroari once again. 'This made the tears run from my eyes,' Barbosa Rodrigues is reported to have said. 'I saw how those who sought civilisation were greeted with fire and sword, and sacrificed.'

Like so many who would follow him in attempting to make contact with isolated indigenous peoples, Barbosa Rodrigues was an incurable optimist. Undeterred, he returned to the Waimiri-Atroari in 1884. John Hemming describes what happened next:

A naval launch was stationed at the mouth of the Jauaperi to prevent entry by adventurers who might wreck his attempted pacification, while Barbosa Rodrigues bravely paddled up the river in a canoe, with an armed escort, a captured Atroari boy interpreter, and plenty of presents. After a few days he sighted Indians on the banks. 'His arrival was greeted by murderous cries. The Indians rushed down to the small beach where his boat had landed. Stone axes were brandished at the head of the audacious traveller. But he impassively presented his peace offerings to these furious men: brightly coloured cloth, knives and mirrors.' The attraction of trade goods and a conciliatory approach were immediately successful; the shouting abated and Barbosa

Rodrigues was led to the Atroari huts as a friend. A few days later, peace was concluded. The Brazilian promised that the Indians would no longer be molested; they in turn promised to forget past injuries.

Pax Jauaperi was, of course, too good to be true. He encouraged the Waimiri-Atroari to abandon many of their traditions, and he built rectangular huts to replace their communal buildings. He also tried to turn them into farmers. Any official peace meant little. The Waimiri-Atroari continued to raid boats and settlements such as Moura, and the settlers and soldiers raided far up the Jauaperi. When the Waimiri-Atroari evicted rubber-tappers from their lands in 1905, the governor of Amazonas, Constantino Nery, again sent soldiers upriver to wreak their vengeance. They killed 283 Indians, burning many of them alive, capturing nineteen. As John Hemming reports, 'These wretches were kept in the barracks of the military police. Many citizens of Manaus recalled seeing them sadly wandering down to the riverfront to gaze at the forests on the far bank.'

There was, it seemed, no way back, and the Waimiri-Atroari retreated into their forests. For the next 70 years, they killed anyone who tried to enter. For a time in 1967 and 1968, they tolerated the presence of Father Antônio Calleri of the Consolata Order when he tried to set up a mission on Waimiri-Atroari land. No one knows what happened, but in 1969, the Indians killed Father Calleri and the seven nuns who were with him. A few years later, they allowed Gilberto Figueiredo Pinto to enter their lands and make contact. Figueiredo Pinto was a celebrated *sertanista*, one of the pioneers of FUNAI, the Brazilian government's Indian agency charged with making contact with isolated tribes. But they killed him as well in 1974 when he tried to convince them they should allow the government to build the BR-174.

A 2013 report by the Truth Commission of Amazonas State found that during the building of the BR-174, agents of the military government killed or caused the disappearance of at least 2000 Waimiri-Atroari. 'There are no old Waimiri-Atroari Indians,' Clark told me. 'They're all young.' It was true. Of the 332 Waimiri-Atroari who survived in 1983, 216 were under twenty years old. The authorities and their road-builders wiped out 89 per cent of the Waimiri-Atroari population, including entire generations. It was one of the more successful campaigns of genocide in modern history.

Awed by what I'd seen and heard here at Xixuaú, I wondered out loud if Clark or Valdemar could take me to visit the Waimiri-Atroari. I was uncomfortable even to ask—any such intrusion onto their lands was voyeuristic, and I knew it. But perhaps if I went with Clark . . . By way of an answer, Clark told me the story of a Protestant pastor who'd gone fishing and looking for turtles upriver. He ignored the signs that said, 'Indian Reserve: No Entry' and entered Waimiri-Atroari lands.

According to Clark, the Waimiri-Atroari caught him and sank his boat. Then they beat him, 'shot him with arrows in different parts of his body, and as a finishing touch rolled him across ground littered with the horrible thorns of the Joari palm tree'. Then they abandoned him by the riverside. 'He had to walk for two days to get to the next river, up to the Xiparina, and we had to take him downriver because his legs were all swollen up. That put the fear of God in him.'

The Waimiri-Atroari and Clark weren't best buddies, but they got on fine. They shared many of the same goals, and the fear engendered by incidents like this worked for both, as Clark wrote in his journal.

> Stories that the Indians were threatening the same treatment to anybody else caught entering their area began to circulate and, somehow, they came to include our area as well. Everybody soon believed that entering our reserve would cause the wrath of the Indians as much as entering their reserve. Of course, I quietly cultivated this belief . . . We did have interests in common and for them it was very good to have us acting as a cushion prior to their land, a buffer zone where already the intruders could be caught and turned back. This was a great help to us in defending the Xixuaú . . . Of course, there were still a number of local men from the river willing to pilot these boats and fish for their owners in exchange for a small amount of money or even just for some alcohol. But they were all terrified of the Indians and that kept us safe as well.

Clark had been to the Waimiri-Atroari control point, which is some 40 minutes up the Jauaperi from Xixuaú. The control point was, Clark said, always attended by armed Indians, watching for intruders from a big round hut on the river-bank. Clark had even been beyond, and into the villages of the Waimiri-Atroari reserve. But even Clark knew that there were limits to his access. 'I couldn't go there just to say hello. I would have to be going there because there was something serious that we needed to talk about. Which is what they do when they come here. They don't come here just to have a coffee. They don't even drink coffee. They don't want relationships with people from the outside.'

Clark knew this from experience. Even Clark's two daughters had never visited Waimiri-Atroari land, and he knew that even asking could get him in trouble.

'A very, very rich Italian friend of mine who came here and helped me a lot asked me once if I would *please* ask the Indians if he could visit them,' Clark told me. 'It was in the early years, about three years into the time we'd been here. I made the mistake of asking them, and they were really, *really* upset about that request. Which I would *never* do again.'

So they said no?

'Absolutely! In no uncertain terms. They gave me a real bollocking.' Clark laughed sheepishly. 'I got really told off. I will never do it again. So many television companies have asked me. And I'm not even going to ask them, because I just know what the answer is going to be.'

Clark had one last story to tell.

'One day, this little canoe with a thatched covering on half of it turned up here. In it was this *huge* guy from Norway—he must have been at least six foot five—and this gamey little tourist guide from Manaus. This Norwegian guy had paid the guide to take him to see an Indian tribe. And this guy had decided that he was going to take this Norwegian to go and see the Waimiri-Atroari. And so they stopped here on their way up.'

Clark tried to warn them off. The Norwegian was adamant. The guide didn't want to disappoint his client. So off they went.

'About two days later, they're back here again and they're completely black and blue, and they were swollen. They'd gotten up to the floating platform of the Indian village. The Indian village is a little bit further inland—there's a path down to the river. They got past the control post and got to the port of the village. Then the Indians came upon them, tied up the guide, put the Norwegian on his knees, and beat the shit out of both of them. And then they just came back down here, all beaten up.'

There was a brief coda to the story. A week later, Ze Maria, a Waimiri-Atroari chief whom Clark knew, came down to berate Clark for having let the Norwegian and his guide enter Waimiri-Atroari land. Clark assured him that it had nothing to do with him. Clark placated the irate chief, but he had got the message.

We never spoke again about visiting the Waimiri-Atroari.

It can be tempting to see Brazil's indigenous peoples as victims of the country's modern history, and in many ways they are. But there lurks in Clark's stories a more complicated, more hopeful truth. The nineteenth-century invasion of their territory by soldiers and slavers, the massacres and epidemics that accompanied the building of the BR-174, the excision of vast tracts of forest in what had been Waimiri-Atroari territory to build the failed Balbina Dam—these events nearly wiped the Waimiri-Atroari from the map and from history.

But they're still there, driving intruders from their land as they have been doing for nearly two centuries. Although always vulnerable, they are masters of one of Brazil's largest indigenous reserves, a territory with one of the lowest population densities on the planet. Some observers believe that small groups of uncontacted Waimiri-Atroari, who have never seen outsiders, may still roam the interior of the vast reserve. The Waimiri-Atroari have stared down the Roraima state government, which has tried in vain to overturn the nightly closure of the 120-kilometre-stretch of the BR-174 that passes through Waimiri-Atroari land. And they have withstood incursions and misinformation campaigns by government operatives and mining companies, even turning some to their advantage. In late 1996, in protest at low royalties and the pollution of the Alalaú River, 110 armed Waimiri-Atroari warriors blocked a mine-access road and the 200 trucks that passed along the road every day. Forced to negotiate, the Paranapanema mining company granted the Waimiri-Atroari a 100 per cent increase in royalties, to around US$30,000 (A$40,000) per month. That figure later increased to US$50,000 (A$63,000). The Waimiri-Atroari also negotiated a massive compensation payout for the Balbina Dam debacle.

It is well known how the Villas Boas brothers from São Paulo famously assisted the peoples of the Xingu in setting up the Amazon's first indigenous reserve in 1961. Less known is the role played by another outsider from São Paulo in helping the Waimiri-Atroari. José Porfírio Fontenele de Carvalho moved to the Amazon in the 1960s and never really left. In the aftermath of the massacres in the 1970s and 1980s, he helped shepherd the Waimiri-Atroari towards financial independence by constructing a legal and banking framework that protected them and their future.

There is the danger in these stories—of Orlando and Claudio Villas Boas, of José Porfírio Fontenele de Carvalho, even of Clark himself—that white saviours become the heroes in the battles to save the Amazon. They are heroes and their stories are important. But these men are notable in part because it is the outside world—the whites, if you like—who have nearly destroyed the Amazon. It is indigenous people who have paid the highest price for the destruction. They are also the ones who have done the most to reverse it.

Porfírio and Clark were friends. 'Porfírio died about a year ago,' Clark told me in Xixuaú in 2018. 'He basically helped make the Waimiri independent, not that most of them worry about money. They've got an aeroplane, they've got outboards, they've got jeeps and lorries on the road. And they control *everything*, absolutely everything. And they're nobody's fool. Nobody can fool them.' Thanks to the proceeds of the resources extracted from their land, the Waimiri-Atroari run schools and health posts in every one of their villages, all staffed by trained Waimiri-Atroari teachers and nurses. Out of the ashes, the Waimiri-Atroari have somehow made it work.

To illustrate how they've done this, Clark told a story, as he often did.

Throughout the first decade of the 21st century, commercial fishing boats were pushing further upriver with each passing year. More often than not, these forays were illegal. At best they violated the tangled web of fishing agreements and regulations that control access to the waterways north of the Rio Negro. At worst, the crews did what they wanted and to hell with the Indians, and who was going to stop them anyway? Whenever Clark and his companions saw the fishing boats, they would go out and ask them to leave. Some left. But most kept right on fishing. Some even warned off Clark and Valdemar and the others with guns. When that happened, Clark would head upriver to the Waimiri-Atroari control point. Not long after, Waimiri-Atroari warriors, often in war paint for full effect, would stream downriver and send the fishing boats scurrying back downstream. 'Everybody's terrified,' Clark remembered with a laugh. 'The Indians terrify everybody.'

Something had to give, and on one occasion in 2007, crew on a commercial fishing boat north of Xixuaú pointed a shotgun at a Waimiri-Atroari canoe. They weren't technically on Waimiri-Atroari land, but nor were the fishermen supposed to be there. Such niceties mattered little. The Indians had had enough and everyone knew it. The fishermen fled downriver, stopping only long enough to warn the villagers of the upper Jauaperi that the Indians were headed their way, primed to massacre every *caboclo* man, woman and child they could find. Panic spread. Two-thirds of the people in Xixuaú grabbed whatever belongings they could find and they, too, fled for their lives.

Daubed in war paint, the Indians did venture down to Xixuaú the next day. But massacre was not their purpose. After making enquiries about the fishing boats they had encountered the day before, they returned upriver, but not before they made a bold statement that Clark later described. 'The Indians took the signposts that said "Indian land" and relocated them 12 kilometres downstream and across the Jauaperi to right where Xixuaú ends. So that became the Indian Reserve.'

Was that legal?

'They did it. And because they had good representation, they then claimed that traditionally they used that land and were allowed to use that land. They just moved the signposts, *then* made the claim.'

It was an incendiary act, one whose repercussions could, if left unchallenged, have far-reaching consequences across the Amazon. That it was done in Roraima, one of Brazil's most conservative states with a history of pro-ranching, anti-indigenous policies, only made things worse.

'The government of Roraima went *ape-shit*,' Clark said, smiling with pleasure, mimicking the politicians: '"These fucking Indians are taking over another massive swathe of land"—because it *is* a massive swathe of land. It's 12 kilometres on the river, but it closes off this entire other river, and a hell of a lot of land there. I mean, it's not a small area. The politicians of Roraima went crazy.'

The response was loud and full of indignant bluster, but the signs remained where the Waimiri-Atroari had moved them. Roraima took the Waimiri-Atroari to Brazil's Supreme Federal Court in Brasília. But the case dragged on as the Waimiri-Atroari simply refused to move their signs.

By 2010, with the Workers' Party mired in scandal and

then-president Dilma Rousseff eager to stem the collapse in the government's popularity—support for indigenous rights is rarely a vote-winner in Brazil—the federal government decided to act. Under the pretext of reasserting government control over its frontiers in the Amazon, the government sent frigates and warships up and down the major rivers of the Amazon basin. The politicians of Roraima saw their chance.

Soon, two military corvettes powered up the Jauaperi. Uniformed soldiers peered out at the forest. Helicopters awaited instructions on deck. Mounted guns pointed into the trees. The two corvettes came to a stop on the Jauaperi just outside Xixuaú. The commander of the whole operation came into Xixuaú in a smaller launch more suited to the narrow entrance into the lagoon, while helicopters circled overhead.

It was something of a shock to Clark and the others in the small community. 'We were totally surprised. We just woke up one day and they were here. It was high water, obviously. Otherwise, they couldn't have got up here. They're impressive big things, corvettes.'

The commander called everyone together and told them that they were here to protect the frontiers of Brazil and to move the Indian signposts back to their original locations. Most in the community thought this a very good thing indeed. 'Here, most of the people hate the Indians,' Clark told me, 'and they're like, "Yeah, go and kick 'em out! Go get 'em! Go get 'em back!"' Clark urged caution upon the commander, warning that the Waimiri-Atroari were not easily cowed.

The next morning, the commander left the corvettes anchored in the river outside Xixuaú and headed upriver in two large launches. With him was a lean but formidable fighting force. If Clark and the people at Xixuaú hadn't known the corvettes were coming, the Waimiri-Atroari certainly did. Clark took up the story.

'The commander and his men went up there. They got to the very edge of the reserve—which is where I always go to—to the very first Indian post up there. It's maybe 20 kilometres from here. They're up there in the middle of the river, and on the riverbank there are all these naked Indians, a lot of them, with war paint and with bows and arrows, pointing at them.'

The launches eased nervously to a stop, unsure what to do next. Everyone held their breath. The Indians were immobile, unreadable. Someone had to do something, so the commander signalled to the other launch to stay where it was and ordered his launch slowly towards the riverbank. In Portuguese, he announced: 'We represent the Brazilian government. We're from the armed forces. We're here because we want to talk to you about the fact that you have moved 12 kilometres downriver.' Silence. Then one of the Waimiri-Atroari stepped forward and replied, 'We'll meet you tomorrow at Chris Clark's place.'

What the commander and his men didn't know, and what the Waimiri-Atroari told Clark later, was that the Indians were ready for war. They had fully expected that the two launches were there to launch an attack. And what the commander and his men couldn't see was that the armed Indians who lined the riverbank were a mere fraction of the Waimiri-Atroari fighting force that was there to defend their land. Behind the first wall of trees was something close to the entire Waimiri-Atroari nation, prepared for one final stand, ready to fight to the death in defending their land. 'They were going to fight,' said Clark, shaking his head. 'They were totally ready to fight with their bows and arrows.'

In Xixuaú village across the lagoon from Clark's hut, there is a large, open-sided *maloca*, or communal building, with a high thatched roof. And so it was that the following day, 40 navy personnel in full military uniform sat on one side of the *maloca*'s long table, and across from them sat fifteen Waimiri-Atroari Indians who'd travelled down to Xixuaú that morning. At the head of the table sat Clark to preside over peace negotiations between two angry nations.

The naval commander spoke first. He thanked the Waimiri-Atroari for coming. He told them that the navy came in peace. He told them that they had come to talk about the signposts that the Indians had moved downriver. He said that the government of Roraima had asked them to come here to find a solution to this problem.

Clark signalled to Ze Maria, the chief and nominated speaker for the Waimiri-Atroari that it was his turn to speak.

'It's good to see the authorities of Brazil in the area,' Ze Maria began. 'There are a lot of things you can do to help us in this area, to help the people, to help us make things better in this area,' he continued. Then he paused. 'But we're not here to talk about the signposts. If you want to talk about this issue, get in touch with our legal team.' And with that, they stood up, all fifteen of them, turned around, and left. End of meeting. They walked down to the riverbank and boarded their boats, bound for Waimiri-Atroari land.

It took all of Clark's self-control not to smile at the time, he said; now he laughed when he thought of it. 'These military guys were just sitting there, shit-faced. They didn't know what to do.' Short of going to war, the navy had no idea what to do next. Muttering darkly about consequences, they hurried to their corvettes and headed south. They were never seen in Xixuaú again.

To this day, the signposts remain by the river just outside Xixuaú, right where the Waimiri-Atroari left them. The land is effectively theirs.

After telling me this story, Clark sat quietly for a long time, smiling.

'Okay, I'm ready,' he said. 'It's time to tell you how I got here. It's time to tell my story.'

# Book Two

# 7

# The Early Years

*1960–1976*

On 14 October 1960, Christopher Julian Clark was born into the damp, grey wool sock that can be Glasgow in mid-autumn. Back then, the Amazon didn't need saving.

No one really knows how big the Amazon was at the time. Most likely it ranged across more than four million square kilometres. In an area more than half the size of Australia, there were just 200 kilometres of paved roads. Many of these were in the cities, in Manaus and Belém, with their faded mansions and idle ports built during the rubber boom six decades earlier. Only rivers penetrated the forest's interior. Many indigenous peoples remained uncontacted and uncorrupted by the world and its ways. And the process of deforestation had yet to begin in earnest. When Clark was born, the Amazon was intact. Or as John Hemming, put it, 'the world's richest ecosystem' was still 'a pristine paradise'. In 1959, a year before Clark's birth, Peter

Matthiessen arrived in the Amazon. It was a century since the celebrated naturalists Henry Walter Bates and Richard Spruce had visited. 'The few large towns excepted,' Matthiessen wrote, 'the traveller on the Amazon sees almost precisely what these men saw a century ago.'

The Amazon was then, and remains, the world's largest rainforest. Half of all rainforest on the planet lay, and still lies, within the Amazon. Sixty per cent of it is within Brazil's borders. The flow of the Amazon river is greater than the world's next eight largest rivers *combined*, including the Nile, Yangtze, Mississippi and Congo. Its volume is sixty times greater than that of the Nile. It is five times wider, and five times deeper, than the Mississippi.

Six decades after Chris Clark was born, precious little else remained the same. One-fifth of the Amazon rainforest, perhaps more, had disappeared. In the heart of what was once dense tropical rainforest there were now roads and cities. And an area of the Amazon larger than New South Wales and Victoria combined had been transformed into cattle ranches and soybean plantations.

All of this happened during Chris Clark's lifetime.

Brazil's national planners talked about taming the Amazon long before 1960. They just hadn't got around to it yet. In 1930, Brazil's military, led by Getúlio Vargas, seized power in a coup d'état. He became the first to demand a 'March to the West'. In 1940, in Manaus, he called on Brazilians 'to conquer and dominate the valleys of the great equatorial torrents, trans-forming their blind force and their extraordinary fertility into disciplined energy'. Another senior military figure promised to 'flood the Amazon forest with civilisation'. Vargas was the first to see Brazil's undeveloped frontier as what John Hemming has called 'a safety valve for rural unrest', as a way to buy off Brazil's vast pool of rural poor. Vargas's successor, Juscelino Kubitschek, built a new national capital, Brasília, in what was then (but is no longer) the Amazon. Connecting the new capital to the rest of Brazil was the Belém–Brasília Highway, the 'Jaguar Highway'. It became the first major road through the Brazilian Amazon. The new capital and the new highway opened in 1960, the year Chris Clark was born.

When Clark was four years old, the military again seized power in Brazil. The military has always been at the heart of Brazil's relationship with the Amazon, seeing in it complex questions of national pride and national security. Their catchcry for the Amazon came to be *ocupar para não entregar* (occupy so as not to surrender). To Brazil's military men, the Amazon was an affront: how could 60 per cent of Brazil's territory be uncharted, beyond their control and, far worse, unproductive? And to these uniformed men who considered it their duty to lead and control the nation, it just wasn't right that, at the time of Clark's birth in 1960, 96.5 per cent of Brazil's population of 70 million people had to crowd into only 40 per cent of the land. Just 2.5 million people lived in the remaining 60 per cent of Brazilian territory, in the Amazon. Many of these were Indians. There was nothing subtle about the way that the military sold their plans for the Amazon to the wider population.

As one general put it, 'Only when we are sure that every corner of the Amazon is settled by real Brazilians, not Indians, will we be able to say that the Amazon belongs to us.' Another leader called the Amazon 'a land without people for a people without land'. To change all of this, they began felling trees and clearing land. Soon, they were eating away at the Amazon's southern and then eastern flanks, in the states of Mato Grosso, Goiás, Pará and Rondônia. They pushed back the frontier.

Roads were key to this growing devastation. When Clark turned ten, so too did the Jaguar Highway between Belém and Brasília. In its first decade, the population in the territory through which the road passed grew by 2000 per cent, to two million. Where once there had been ten towns there were now 120. Roads made the Amazon accessible for settlers and enabled them to get their crops and cattle to market. These new migrants didn't live in the forest. They cleared it, and the Amazon began to shrink.

Soon enough, the authorities began to build another road across the Amazon. The BR-364 ran from Cuiabá in Mato Grosso state to Porto Velho on the Madeira River in Rondônia. John Hemming described the BR-364 as 'the artery for the greatest migration into virgin territory in South American history'. It was, he wrote, 'notorious as the greatest destroyer of rain forests'. With the Jaguar Highway, it formed part of what he called 'an arc of deforestation'.

Roads killed more than forests. They also enabled genocide. After the arrival of Europeans in the sixteenth century, colonial armies and the slavers they enabled had wiped out indigenous communities along the main rivers. Many Indian groups retreated deep into the most remote forests and survived into the twentieth century. A 7000-page report published in the 1960s found that the Indian Protection Service, set up to 'protect' indigenous Amazonians in Brazil in 1910, had overseen mass murder, torture and slavery. The Indian Protection Service and those they enabled, the report revealed, stole Indian land, poisoned indigenous children in the forest, and forced Indian women into prostitution. They also deliberately infected indigenous communities with diseases. By one estimate, one million Indians lived in the Amazon at the dawn of the twentieth century. By 1960, barely 200,000 remained. The outcry when these figures were released was far-reaching, and the new FUNAI agency replaced the Indian Protection Service. In 1969, as a direct response to the report, the international NGO Survival International was formed to advocate on behalf of indigenous people worldwide.

The rate of road-building accelerated. In 1971, Brazil's military president Emílio Médici arrived in the region on a state visit. Appalled by the poverty he encountered, he ordered the construction of the Trans-Amazonian Highway—the Rodovia Transamazônica or BR-230. On 27 September 1972, less than three weeks before Clark's twelfth birthday, the first stretch of this famous highway opened. The large-scale influx of settlers that followed was less a by-product of the road-building fervour than the road's reason for existence. Although it remains to this day a highway in name only, unpaved for most of its 4000 kilometres and impassable for much of the year, the highway was a statement of intent. It was also a harbinger of everything that followed.

By 1974, the authorities completed 2232 kilometres of the Transamazônica, from the Tocantins to the Madeira. If nothing else, it was a remarkable feat of engineering, the equivalent of forging a forest trail from Lisbon to Vienna, or from Melbourne to Mackay. By the end of the same year, a road connected Porto Velho with Manaus, deep in the Amazon. Botanist David Campbell carried out urgent studies of the flora and fauna along this road's path in 1974. The scientists slept in their cars because jaguars roamed their camps. One per cent of all plants they found were new to science. These studies were rare witness testaments to a fast-disappearing world. 'Some of the plant species we collected have never been seen since,' Campbell wrote, 'and it is unlikely that they ever will be seen again. Our collections will be the only evidence they existed.'

With each of these roads, the pattern was the same. First, the main access roads cut a primary path through the forest. From these roads, minor roads branched out. Over time, the view from above came to resemble a fish skeleton. Before long, the destruction of the Amazon took on momentum and became irreversible. Up to 80 per cent of deforestation in the Amazon would take place within 50 kilometres of major roads.

The Amazon was disappearing. By 1980, bulldozers and chainsaws had cleared nearly thirteen million hectares (130,000 square kilometres) of Amazon rainforest. And for what? Despite projects costing US$2.9 billion, and despite nearly three-quarters of this forest having been cleared for cattle pasture, the Amazon remained a net importer of beef. A decade later, the conservative Brazilian news magazine *Veja*—no friend of environmentalists—admitted: 'Intensive occupation promoted by the government in Brazilian Amazonia has been a disaster. It devastated an area greater than Japan to yield less than the national product of Suriname. Over 30 million hectares [300,000 square kilometres] of trees were uprooted to give way to a hundred ruinous cattle projects.'

No one bothered to tell the impoverished settlers that the Amazon's outward signs of fertility were a ruse. The Amazon's soil is almost universally poor and unsuited to agriculture. Newly exposed to relentless sunlight, Amazonian soils will consume themselves and, without replenishing rains, turn to sand and dust. And this is to say nothing of the region's challenging climate, and its proliferation of insects and parasites. As Andrew Revkin has noted, 'For the most part, the millions of dollars that were poured into resettlement and water projects and roads heading west into the Amazon benefited only construction contractors, real estate speculators, and corrupt government officials.' Or, to put it another way, 'All of the government's projects resulted in little more than the destruction of great tracts of forest.'

It wasn't just settlers who flooded into the Amazon. Soon, the Amazon's roads and rivers filled with *garimpeiros* (gold prospectors) chasing the dream of a goldmining boom in the rainforest. The newcomers, most of them without any legal right to work the land, invaded Indian territory. They brought with them a new wave of disease and death, of pollution and deforestation.

～

A world away from the Amazon, Chris Clark was the third child of Barbara Clark (nee Brown) and Colin Wilfred Clark. He had an older brother and sister and would ultimately be one of six children. His father was a publisher of children's books. Clark's mother took charge of the home. In Clark's telling of his childhood, it was a comfortable, unremarkable middle-class existence. 'We were not well off but nor were we poor,' he remembered. 'We had a nice big house and plenty of room and I recall no suffering or privations. It was one of those typical upwardly mobile families of the '60s.'

Clark did well at school, although Colin Clark's job required the family to move back and forth between London and Glasgow. Every time the family moved, Chris and his siblings had to begin over. For a child, this could be traumatic. 'I remember very clearly moving from London to Glasgow at around eleven and being traumatised because I was in love with a girl called Kathleen. I spent the first six months in Scotland not sleeping at night and driving my parents crazy.' Fifty years later, he could still remember this Kathleen's address in South Ruislip, which was formerly in Middlesex, now part of Greater London. He even named his eldest daughter Cathleen, in honour of his first childhood love.

Paul, Chris's older brother, remembered that back in Middlesex there wasn't always enough food to go around. The move to Glasgow in 1971 significantly improved the family's financial position. In Glasgow, Colin became managing director of the children's division at the publisher William Collins, where he had once worked as an apprentice. At the same time, life in Glasgow was a shock to the young Chris

Clark. After a relatively sheltered life just outside London, he found himself thrust into the sometimes terrifying public schoolyards of early 1970s Glasgow. Something of a sensitive soul, Chris was, according to his elder brother Paul, a little traumatised to begin with by the coarse language and the unpredictable violence of playground life. Their parents even took Chris to see a psychologist. Nobody's fool, he soon learned to defend himself.

It was this uprooting of his young life, Clark told me, that nurtured in him a certain restlessness: 'Moving about a lot made it hard to put down roots and develop long-term friendships with people.' He also came from a family of travellers and adventurers and those who'd otherwise spent time overseas. His great-grandparents lived for a time in colonial India; one of his great-grandparents was a bandmaster in the British army. His maternal grandparents lived in South Africa during the Boer War. During World War I, German poison gas blinded one of Clark's grandfathers. Shrapnel crippled another. Perhaps this family history of time spent on foreign shores encouraged him to seek out a life far from home and family. But that may not have been the only reason.

One family member would, decades later, describe Colin Clark as 'the sweetest person on earth'. Chris himself counted his father as one of the rocks, one of the moral anchors, in his life.

Clark's mother was a very different story. One family member remembered how Colin Clark 'spent 60 years of his life with someone next to him, telling him "Shush, Colin! Shush, Colin!" He didn't really have a chance to have a will, or to say things in the family.' Barbara was adopted and had been raised as she would one day raise her own children: with little joy, uncomfortable with physical shows of affection and, at the heart of everything, with a strict interpretation of the moral codes of the Catholic Church. Upon reaching adulthood, Barbara Clark went looking for her biological family. But hers was not like a life you see in the movies. Her quest ended almost before it began when she learned that they had died some years earlier. Although her life appeared happy enough to any casual observer—she was careful to cultivate an outward appearance of a quiet and uncontroversial family life—she rarely showed any joy, and she certainly never spread it.

Like a minor character in a Charles Dickens novel, Barbara Clark filled the space and ruled her family's life. She controlled the family home with steely, suffocating discipline. She was an old-school disciplinarian, dour and controlling. When she was angry, her displeasure was cold and hard. She rarely raised her voice but nor did she have to: everyone knew the consequences. Barbara Clark was certainly not averse to meting out physical punishments. On one occasion, she slapped Chris so hard that he cried for two hours. But her silence could be just as frightening. When peace reigned, it was usually because, according to one family member, 'We would all just shut up because we didn't want to argue with her.' Dinner-table manners and etiquette were important and were rigidly enforced: *Don't* put your elbows on the table. *Don't* chew with your mouth open. *Don't . . . Don't . . .* If they misbehaved, the children were sent to bed and confined to their rooms for the rest of the day, regardless of the hour. They were expected to attend the local

Catholic church every Sunday, no excuses. The family gave thanks to God over every meal.

As an adult, Clark would write of his parents as

> ...failing to understand that people do not always take kindly to being told what to do and being bossed about. Mine are members of that class of parents who always see their offspring as children and believe inherently that they know best. They gave no leeway in the little things like time of bed, table manners, listening to music, and, most of all, every one of their children's, and later their grandchildren's, friends were viewed as intruders, to be put in their place at every opportunity.

Barbara Clark knew from the beginning that Christopher, her third child, was different. She always called him 'my little sunshine'. She recorded a hagiographic film about him on a visit to the Amazon when she was well into her eighties. Even so, there were times when Clark felt as if he had been born into the wrong family. While still an adolescent, he developed a passion for escaping into the northern wilds of Scotland, hitch-hiking into and camping in the thinly populated Highlands. Sometimes he went with friends. Sometimes he travelled alone. With each passing trip, he became more self-sufficient. It was his first real taste of freedom, and with each expedition, he became more eager to see what lay beyond the horizon.

When a much older man, Clark would revisit one of the houses in which he spent some years during his teens, in Riverdale, near Camberley, south-west of London. As another family member remembered it, it was the kind of neighbour-hood 'where they all have the same houses, same kids, same clothes, same everything. It was a London suburban neigh-bourhood—rich people, private schools, those little villas with green grass, and nothing ever happens. People just go insane because nothing ever happens.' Pointing to that house decades later, Clark would tell a family member: 'This was my prison.'

In a hurry, Clark finished his O-Levels at fourteen years old, and his A-Levels at sixteen. He was done with school two years ahead of schedule. Clark left home soon after. Some say that was what happened in those days in the UK—that many young people left home while still in their teens. But one day, Clark just snapped. He couldn't take living under Barbara Clark's roof anymore. So he bought a scooter and left the family home near London, and rode all the way to Scotland. He never went home again.

# 8

# Into the Forest

*1976–1984*

Christopher Clark was not destined for a quiet and sedentary Scottish life. Although there is nothing to suggest that he made the connection in his own mind at the time, Clark headed abroad at the precise historical moment when the destruction of the Amazon was gaining frightening momentum. Through his father's contacts, Clark, aged just sixteen, began what was supposed to be a six-month internship in the foreign rights department at Fabbri Editori, a publishing company in Milan.

Languages always came easily to Clark. His Italian became so good so quickly that he stayed on to translate into English a collector's edition on Italian arts and crafts. Soon, he had his own office. He may not have known what was happening in the Amazon, but he was briefly caught up in the tumult of the Middle East. In 1978, Fabbri Editori lost vast sums of money during the Islamic Revolution in Iran when the Ayatollah Khomeini tore up publishing and printing contracts signed by the Shah of Iran and refused to pay the country's debts.

Chastened by events in Iran, Fabbri's foreign rights director at the time turned away a Syrian emissary working on behalf of a Middle Eastern publishing company. Staff ushered the Syrian into Clark's office and the two men got to talking. Whatever Clark said, it clearly made an impression. Two weeks after their first meeting, the Syrian called Clark to offer him the job as foreign rights director of a new publishing company called Dolphin Publishers, operating out of Milan. Clark said yes.

The company where Clark worked was a microcosm of the Arab world at the time. The intellectuals behind Dolphin were Syrians. The money came from investors from oil-rich Kuwait, Saudi Arabia and the Gulf States. And the machine labourers in Milan—Dolphin operated out of one of Silvio Berlusconi's earliest development areas, the Colonia Montsesi—were mostly Egyptian and Palestinian immigrants. Clark travelled the world, attending book fairs in Frankfurt, Los Angeles, London and elsewhere, buying the Arab-language rights to books from global publishers. It was an extraordinary opportunity for such a young man. 'Suddenly I was earning an incredible salary. I had my own secretary. I was getting sent around the world, staying in five-star hotels.' It could have set him up for life.

The temptation for a man, barely out of adolescence, to build a glamorous life where he could name his price must have been considerable. But Clark, still the restless one who had loved nothing more than disappearing on his own into the Scottish Highlands, was unimpressed: 'I was uncomfortable. The Hiltons, the Sheratons—wherever you go, you could be anywhere. It really annoyed me to go to a city I'd never been to before and stay in exactly the same place as I'd stayed in the last city I was in. There was absolutely no difference at all.'

A way out for Clark soon arrived. At the 1982 Frankfurt Book Fair, the Canadian arm of publisher Hodder & Stoughton made Clark an offer he couldn't refuse. They would pay him a lucrative salary if he translated an Italian encyclopaedia into English for them. All he had to do was send in a certain amount of work every three months for the next three years. Clark was confident he could complete each batch of work in just three weeks. The rest of the time he would be free to do as he liked.

Life was good. He had a steady income. He was no longer tied to a desk. And he had begun sharing his world with a new girlfriend, Anna Bonari, whose family lived in Tuscany, where they spent increasing amounts of time. It opened up a whole new world of possibilities and Clark took full advantage of them.

He and his girlfriend bought two round-the-world tickets and spent the next two years travelling the world. They had no fixed itinerary, spent very little money, and stayed in a place as long as they wanted before moving on. Gone were the five-star hotels. All Clark needed to be happy was his portable typewriter, his girlfriend and a constant slideshow of new adventures. Near the end of their journey, they landed in Brazil.

$\sim$

It was an exciting time to be in Brazil. The military had seized power in 1964, and they still ruled Brazil when Clark visited twenty years later. But the days of military rule were drawing to a close and the country stood on the brink of historic change. Clark and Bonari attended the last truly authentic street carnival in Rio de Janeiro—in 1985 it moved from the streets to the custom-built Sambadrome, and samba nostalgics remember the 1984 swansong with great fondness. Clark and Bonari tracked north along the coast, stopping in Salvador de Bahía for its own version of Carnival, the Trio Elétrico. There has always been a contrarian streak in Clark, and while neither event was his thing, he enjoyed Salvador's version more than he did the world's most famous street party.

He and Bonari continued north. In a bar in Belém, they met Danish photographer Erik Falk, who was on assignment for the Danish Ministry of Education. Falk had a strong voice and chiselled features and Bonari felt intimidated by this imposing Dane. 'He had a really hard face,' Bonari remembered. Clark, Bonari and Falk together boarded the government passenger ship for the five-day journey upriver to Manaus.

Not all Amazonian river journeys are romantic. Clark and Bonari slept on the couples' deck, where there was space, at least, between the hammocks. Falk was exiled to the section for single men, with hammocks close above and below him, and on either side. In Clark's telling, the food was poor, the bar closed at 10 p.m., and the days seemed to last forever: 'A huge steel boat pushing up the Amazon for five days, stopping in big towns to endlessly load and unload. In some places the river is so wide you can't see the sides. I compare travel along the river

Amazon to saying you have seen the UK by travelling along the M1. If you are lucky, you might glimpse the odd dolphin and parrot, but not much else. To see the Amazon, you need to go to tributaries of tributaries. The main river is really boring. It was a relief to arrive in Manaus.'

To Bonari, the Amazon was just one more adventure in a year of many. On their earlier travels she had wondered if she and Clark could build a life together, perhaps in Indonesia. But as soon as they arrived in Brazil, she had to abandon any such dreams. 'After we arrived in the Amazon, Chris went crazy. He loved it. When we arrived in the Amazon, he was home.'

With other travellers, they rented a boat from an old Argentinian named Miguel and began a series of river journeys up and down the Amazon. On their first excursion, they explored the Solimões—the main branch of the Amazon before it reaches Manaus. Among the travelling party was Baixote Encarnação, who showed them his home terrain of Lago de Campinas, lost in the labyrinth of lakes and rivers so typical of the Solimões west of Manaus. There Clark met Baixote's son Plinho, a man who would later be by Clark's side for many of the most important moments in his life.

Their boat trip up the Solimões was an adventure, but as Clark remembered it, 'there were *millions* of mosquitoes down there. It was *really* uncomfortable'. Locals in Manaus assured them that the Rio Negro, north-west of the city, as a black-water river, was largely free of stinging insects. Clark and his companions journeyed up the Rio Negro as far as the mouth of the Jauaperi River, where Clark met Valdemar, who had a large marijuana plantation. 'Valdemar didn't even know how to sell it,' Clark remembered, laughing at the innocence of the man who would one day become one of his closest friends and collaborators. Valdemar would, of course, be my guide in Xixuaú 34 years later. Valdemar told Clark, 'Give me whatever you want to give me, and I'll give you a few supermarket bags full of marijuana.' As Clark remembered, 'There wasn't a price, or anything like that.'

On these early Amazon journeys, Clark had found some of the people—Falk, Plinho, and Valdemar—who would one day play a critical role in his future. What he didn't know at the time was that he had also found the place that would define him: Clark would go on to spend much of his life many miles up the Jauaperi River.

Upon their return to Manaus, most of the travellers went their separate ways. Even Anna Bonari returned to Italy, but not before the couple had argued spectacularly. They hadn't made up before she left, and their relationship was at a cross-roads. Clark felt torn, but he decided to stay for one more river trip. Young and feeling invincible, he was yet to learn what many before him had discovered to their great peril: that a passion for the Amazon can be a very dangerous thing indeed. The Amazon had him in its grasp. And over the weeks that followed, it very nearly didn't let go.

Clark was looking for one last adventure in the Amazon before returning to Europe, and the opportunity soon presented itself. The Argentinian boat owner, Miguel, whom everyone called 'the Baron', knew someone who worked at the National Institute for Amazonian Research (INPA) and who wanted to sell some land. As Clark remembered it, the land in question was 'in the forest about 300 kilometres east of Manaus, down past Itacoatiara, up to Itapiranga on the Uatumã River.' Clark was interested, and Baixote Encarnação decided to go with them.

To finance the trip, they needed paying passengers, so they approached a party of six Italians in a tourist restaurant in Manaus. Clark promised to show them the real Amazon. They didn't need much convincing. Within an hour they were making plans, and they set out a couple of days later. The party of nine travelled on the Baron's boat down the Amazon, then up the Uatumã. At the last, lonely outpost as they headed north, they convinced an old, one-eyed, one-eared *caboclo* named Ze to be their guide.

The adventure didn't begin well. Ze took the Italians out for a spot of night-fishing, but the overloaded canoe sank. Ze thought it was hilarious. The sodden but otherwise unharmed Italians were not amused.

The next morning, they set out to explore the forest on foot. It was an unwieldy party for forest trails, so they split up. Ze took three Italians, while Clark, Baixote and the Baron took the remainder. Clark and his companions hadn't planned or prepared to walk for long. 'We were just into the forest, going for a walk,' he remembered. They set off with confidence. They weren't going far, after all. They had a little water, and they knew that the river was behind them.

The day turned overcast. Then it started to rain. Baixote started having sharp pains in his stomach. The day quickly unravelled.

In the forest, moods shift without warning. Green tendrils reach for the sun, liana curtains rain down from above, and a wild profusion of greenery surrounds the unwary. It can be suddenly disorienting and claustrophobic. Humidity presses close, smothering and oppressive. Everything seems hostile: the strangler figs; the cries and calls of unseen creatures; the silence, brooding and dark. Impenetrable walls of rank green swallow the trail, where there is one. What the leaf litter conceals doesn't bear thinking about.

Clark and his friends grew uneasy. They had paid attention to their surroundings, and thought that they recognised this tree, that flowering plant, this tangle of vines. Until they didn't. Conscious of all the terrifying creatures that lived there, aware of the perils of getting lost, they tried to anchor their progress by identifying a tree up ahead. Then they arrived where they imagined the tree to be, and all the trees looked the same. They tried to retrace their steps, but nothing was familiar. They tried to get a fix on the direction in which they had been walking, but they couldn't find the sun. And even when they imagined they could glimpse the sun as a navigational point through the canopy high above, in such dense jungle who could say where the sun had been when they set out? If they moved further into the forest, they would be further from the river. If they tried to return the way they'd come, how could they know if they had miscalculated? At first it was annoying, and no one believed that they were really lost. For the first few hours, they half expected the river to appear through the trees at any moment. But the forest had closed behind them, sealing them off from the world.

Some in the party still refused to believe that they might be lost but, deep down, they all knew it. Finally, Baixote admitted that he had no idea where they were. They cursed their stupidity. No one had eaten since breakfast. It was getting dark. And the rain just kept on falling. Even so, they were sure that tomorrow would be different, and it was, after all, an adventure. They built a makeshift shelter in which they spent an uncomfortable night.

The next morning was wet and grey. Baixote was now in great pain. As a veteran of Amazon life, the Baron offered to take over as guide. They set off, confident that the weather would clear, and that they would soon find the others. It rained all day. Tempers frayed. Baixote nearly walked into a vine snake hanging from a tree—one step further and he would have died. The only thing they agreed on was that remaining where they were would solve nothing. No one knew where they were. No one would ever find them. They had to move, to take chances. But which way?

They began by taking calculated guesses, hoping against hope for a familiar sign to regain their bearings, listening for the sound of a flowing river. But rivers in the Amazon are mostly silent, and each time their efforts became more fraught. Soon enough, they began to wander aimlessly. There was no denying that they were lost, and the realisation settled as cold fear in the pits of their stomachs. The adventure had become a nightmare.

They had been trudging through the jungle for the best part of two exhausting days. They were more frightened than hungry, which is just as well because they had nothing to eat. They tried to eat leaves, but they knew nothing of the jungle and its plants. What if some were poisonous? At three o'clock on the second day, they reached the riverbank. They were finally able to drink and to wash. But solving one problem had created another. Baixote thought that the boat was moored upstream. Clark disagreed and thought they should head downriver. The Italians were just miserable. Often the master of understatement, Clark remembered it as 'a really strong experience. You don't know if you're going to get out.' Looking back, he laughed, but at the time it was no joke. They slept by the riverbank.

After another night sleeping out in the open, things were starting to look desperate. They argued. Baixote went upstream. Clark and the Baron decided to go downstream. They all hugged each other before parting company, leaving the Italians by the riverbank and promising to return. If one group were to escape the jungle, they could alert the authorities—wherever they might be—and send out a search party. No one said so, but each of them wondered if they would ever see their friends again. Each was thinking the same thing: *Will any of us get out alive?*

Clark and the Baron tried to follow the riverbank, but the jungle was a tangle of vegetation right to the water's edge. As Clark later told TV presenter Ben Fogle, 'We didn't have anything to eat. It was really hilly terrain, and all swampy in the middle. You had to swim across bits. Millions of mosquitoes. We had to spend the night in the forest.'

They were exhausted. The cigarette lighter died. Unable to make a fire, they remained soaked to the skin. They hadn't eaten in three days. The Baron was violently ill, stepping off the trail at regular intervals to dry-retch into the forest. With darkness approaching, they cut some ferns and lay down. 'We huddled together, cold, wet and exceedingly miserable,' Clark later wrote in his journal. 'The mosquitoes that night were a horde from hell. We actually embraced like lovers in our bed of ferns and at some point, exhaustion overtook me and I fell asleep.'

It got worse.

'I came to, being shoved by the Baron with him hissing at me, "Wake up! Wake up! Listen!"' Clark wrote later. 'It was pitch black and I was groggy from sleep and at first, I couldn't hear a thing. Then I caught a whiff of a pungent aroma that reminded me of my childhood in Glasgow. Glasgow tenements had entrances known as closes, which were often used as public lavatories by passing drunks. These closes led to little communal back yards that were more often than not strewn with junk and home to brigades of street cats who scavenged around in the middens, or bins. It was this that I smelt, and then a soft footfall.'

They were being stalked by a jaguar.

'We both got up and started banging on the tree trunks with the palms of our hands and screaming,' Clark told me, decades later. 'From close by came a throaty, deep growl, and this jaguar just went *rrrrr!*—off into the forest because we screamed at it.'

They didn't sleep again that night, their third in the jungle.

They returned along the riverbank, and found a depressing scene. Baixote had been and gone. The Italians were panicking, and one of the men literally tore out his own hair in anguish. When Baixote finally showed up again, he had developed a nasty lump below his ribcage. Unable to bear cutting trails through the forest any longer, they built a makeshift raft, but at some point the machete, their only tool, slipped from the hand of one of the Italians and sank to the bottom of the river. It was a desperate scene when, in the late afternoon, Clark and the Baron pushed away from shore and began half-drifting, half-swimming down the river.

They had no idea if they were going in the right direction. They were desperately hungry. And not long after setting out, the Baron collapsed and it took all of Clark's strength to keep him from sliding off the raft and drowning. 'I remember the last day,' Clark told me later, 'swimming down the river and thinking I just couldn't face another night in the forest. I just said, "God, if you get me out of here, I'll marry Anna."'

Finally, just before sunset, with the Baron barely conscious and with Clark contemplating another night on the riverbank, Ze, their one-eyed, one-eared guide, found them. He had been searching for them for four days. He was on a final sweep before giving them up for dead. He claimed that God had told him where to look. It took three hours to reach the boat, a couple more to find Baixote and the missing Italians. Miraculously, all of them made it out alive.

The Italians fled. They barely said goodbye. Baixote was rushed to hospital and went straight into surgery for a hernia. Suffering from hypothermia and with fluid on his lungs, the Baron remained in hospital for two months.

That would have been enough Amazon immersion—the

discomfort, the hunger, the fear, the insects, the wild animals—for most people. Many, perhaps most, would have followed the Italians in rushing to leave the Amazon, never to return.

But Clark has always been wired differently. As he remembered it years later, out there in the forest, 'I came closer to dying than ever in my life, before or since . . . Almost everybody who lives here, at some point in their lives, goes through something like this.' For Clark, this experience was anything but a deterrent. 'In certain times of crisis, you learn a lot about yourself and the people you're with. I fell in love with the Amazon during those four days.'

Clark would later keep the promise he made in extremis: he and Anna Bonari married upon Clark's return to Italy. Their marriage would last 23 years. Clark's love affair with the Amazon would last even longer.

# 9

# Trouble in the Forest

*1984–1990*

Clark had survived his first real Amazon adventure and he was eager for more. He returned with his older brother, Paul, in December 1984, and thereafter he travelled to the Amazon whenever he could.

When he wasn't in Brazil, he spent most of his time in Tuscany. He could move between the two in part because he was still earning good money translating the encyclopaedia for Hodder & Stoughton. It also helped that this was the mid-1980s, a time when English travellers and would-be expats were discovering Tuscany's quiet, still-affordable charms. Clark spent two years renovating a beautiful old farmhouse in Tuscany's Val d'Orcia, between Siena and Grosseto. By the time he finished, a steady flow of British investors was passing through the area. It began around Chianti, which soon became known as 'Chianti Shire', Clark remembered, because of the growing number of British expats. Then the phenomenon moved down through Siena and the countryside around Grosseto. Clark spoke Italian like a local. He had close ties to the local community. And he had what I later understood to be an aura of extraordinary competence. Clark was perfectly placed to ride what became one of the Western world's defining lifestyle booms of the 1980s. 'Suddenly, I had all of these foreigners asking me for help.'

Just as suddenly, Clark had himself a business. His first remit was to help wealthy, predominantly British, people find abandoned farmhouses. Then they wanted him to transform these ruins into their dream slices of Tuscan life. In time, Clark made himself indispensable. Many came from prominent families, and Clark connected them with reliable building companies, plumbers, electricians, tilers and the like. He also helped his clients negotiate the Byzantine bureaucratic maze that defined Italy's often-corrupt local governments under then-prime minister Bettino Craxi. Clark had up to seven farmhouses on the go at any one time. On the first day of every month, he did his sums and decided how much money he wanted to earn and how hard he wanted to work. Then he named his price.

Not for the first time, Clark's life could have taken a very different direction. He had escaped the prison of his childhood family home, and he was fast becoming independently wealthy. 'There was a period in my life when I was earning a hell of a lot of money,' he remembered. 'It was easy to make money. I could have been very rich. It's never been a really great problem for me. I've always found a way to do it.'

And perhaps that was the problem: for Clark, making money was not enough of a challenge. 'I got completely bored with that. Money is only a tool. It's nothing more than a screw-driver if you need to screw a screw. But it's not the end.' Just as he had discovered a few years earlier when travelling the world for Dolphin Publishers, he had no aspirations for the kind of European life that such money could buy. 'I needed something more,' he told me.

He'd also come to realise that Italy could not provide the kind of challenge that he craved.

As the owner of his company in Tuscany, Clark could leave it whenever he wanted. With all the money and time that he needed, Clark returned every year to Brazil, sometimes for months at a time.

On each visit to the Amazon, Clark made new friends. One of these, in 1989, was Ypassane (known as Edson), a Tukano Indian who was studying in Manaus. The Tukano inhabit one of Brazil's most remote corners, around the Uaupés River, a tributary of the Rio Negro more than 1000 kilometres north-west of Manaus. Their traditional lands straddle the border with Colombia, and the Tukano move freely between the two countries.

Edson invited Clark to visit the Tukano homeland, many days' journey upriver from Manaus. Clark's Danish friend, Erik Falk, joined the expedition, as did Jon and Jan, a two-man film crew from Denmark's national broadcaster. Together, Clark, the three Danes and Edson sailed from Manaus up the Rio Negro, past the mouth of the Jauaperi, past the provincial city of Barcelos, and on to São Gabriel da Cachoeira. A three-day river journey from Manaus, São Gabriel inhabits a beautiful corner of the Upper Rio Negro, with waterfalls and sandy beaches. Nearby, a striking mountain range named the Bela Adormecida (Sleeping Beauty) rises from the rainforest. Clark described it as 'shaped almost exactly like a reclining woman, with head, breasts, flanks, and legs'. São Gabriel is also the trailhead for Brazil's highest mountain, Pico da Neblina (2994 metres), which is close to Brazil's frontier with Venezuela.

São Gabriel da Cachoeira was a military garrison town. Civilian rule had returned to Brazil in 1985, but in remote corners of the rainforest the army served as the government's proxy—especially near the borders with Venezuela and Colombia. At the time of Clark's arrival in São Gabriel, relations between the Tukano and the army were tense. Neither trusted the other.

Since the 1970s, Brazil's military government had been accusing the Tukano of collaborating with Colombian coca traffickers and with a Colombian guerrilla group known as M-19. In response, Brazil's military occupied the area. The army later withdrew from Tukano tribal areas. But they made no secret of their plans to re-establish a military post on Tukano land. They said it was to guard the frontier with Colombia, as FARC and other guerrillas were active just across the border.

For their part, the Tukano loathed the military presence in north-western Brazil. Any military garrison on their land signalled a bitter loss of independence. The Brazilian authorities felt like a foreign power in these parts, and Tukano communities feared any attempts by the army to regain control and chip away at hard-won Indian autonomy.

FUNAI had granted Clark and his party permission to visit the lands of the Tukano and the Yanomami; the Yanomami are one of the largest indigenous nations of the Amazon, and their battles against government intrusion, settler violence and deforestation have been one of the most prominent stories in the international debate over the future of the Amazon. But the army was a different matter and cared little for FUNAI's permits. Edson and his Tukano friends knew that a travelling party of foreigners with cameras would arouse suspicion among the military there. They decided to spend as little time as possible in São Gabriel. They stayed instead in Camanaus, around 10 kilometres downriver. But the plan fell apart when Jon and Jan became suddenly convinced that their hair was falling out. The Danish broadcasters were, in Clark's telling, singularly out of their depth, and Clark would later laugh at how unprepared they were for travelling in the Amazon back country. They were more suited to 'filming ducks in Denmark' than they were to documenting life in the remote rainforest, Clark liked to say. At the smallest crisis, they went to pieces. They insisted on going to the military hospital in São Gabriel and, as Edson and Clark knew it would, their presence in town alerted the local authorities, who hauled them in for questioning. The town's military commander forbade them from travelling to Indian areas without a permit from the Ministry of Internal Affairs in Brasília. They were ordered to return to Manaus. Disappointed, the travelling party moved into a small hotel in São Gabriel, awaiting their departure back downriver.

A military order would have been enough for most people. But Clark and the Tukano weren't most people and began to plot their escape. At dawn one morning, they snuck out of their hotel and drove north out of town, bound for the Yanomami town of Maturaca, where they hoped to film. They cleared the city's outskirts undetected. Just 15 kilometres up the road, five soldiers with machine guns blocked their path. The soldiers escorted them back to São Gabriel, where a military commander reprimanded Clark, as if he were, in Clark's words, 'a naughty schoolboy'. The soldiers confined them to their hotel. Whenever Clark left the hotel, soldiers followed.

They hadn't given up yet. Edson and the other Tukano hatched a plan and, that night, they spirited Clark and his three Danish companions out of the hotel. Under cover of darkness, they quietly made their way beyond the rapids on the western outskirts of town. There, a Tukano boat was waiting to carry them away up the Rio Negro and on to the Rio Uaupés. By the time day dawned in São Gabriel da Cachoeira, they were long gone. To Clark's regret, the soldiers took out their frustrations on a local Tukano leader named Pedro Machado. They raided his home and roughed him up a little for good measure.

It took a day and a half for the fugitives to reach the main Tukano town of Pari Cachoeira, where a large Salesian Catholic mission lorded it over the settlement. Edson introduced Clark to the priests who ran the mission. Among them was an Italian, a Brazilian, and an Irishman named Father Murphy. Far from being the tagline for a joke, Father Murphy was like something out of a Graham Greene novel. Starved of English-speaking company, and delighted when Clark produced a cassette of

Irish music by The Chieftains, Father Murphy opened his stash of beer and whisky and began to talk.

'He told me how they ran this place,' Clark remembered, no longer laughing at the initial caricature of the Irish whisky priest. 'They divided the boys and girls. They weren't allowed to speak Tukano. They had to learn in Portuguese. If they didn't go to church on Sunday and then came to the Mission sick on Monday, they didn't get any medicine. They only got medicine if they'd been to church.' This wasn't something the church would have been keen to publicise, as Clark well knew. 'He only told me,' Clark later told me, 'because he completely relaxed with me, because we were drinking whisky and beer.'

What Clark heard rings true. Although the Tukano knew nothing of it, in 1910 Pope Pius X granted the Salesians exclusive domain over the Rio Negro; the Salesians were a male Catholic order whose missionaries were active in South America at the time. Their missionaries first reached the Tukano in 1915, and it changed the lives of the Tukano forever. Among the Tukano, 1915 became Year Zero. To this day, they divide their history into the time before and after this first contact. The Salesians became active in the area in 1920 and set up the mission in Pari Cachoeira in 1945 and brought with them the Bible and epidemics, including yellow fever. Otherwise, the Salesians were notorious for establishing what John Hemming has called 'a virtual theocracy in that part of Brazil and neighbouring Colombia'. Hemming also records how 'Salesian fathers ordered the demolition of the magnificent great huts, *malocas*, of the Tukano'. These huts were 'architectural masterpieces, dry and cool in all weathers, spotlessly clean, and with their facades decorated in handsome geometric patterns'. One traveller who visited the early Salesian missions in 1927 described the Tukano *malocas* that the Salesians were so keen to destroy as 'the symbol, the veritable bulwark of the former social order . . . everything in them breathes tradition and independence'. Wherever they went, the Salesians asserted control. They destroyed entire villages and rebuilt them to conform with mission style. They also wiped out any traditional social and cultural norms that might rival the teachings of the church. Yes, the Salesians offered Tukano children a church education. But they enrolled only those children taken from their parents and housed in boarding schools under strict clerical control. The children could only visit their families during church-prescribed holiday periods.

Clark was appalled, scarcely able to believe that such practices survived into the 1980s. 'It was absolutely awful, and this had been going on since the 1920s. Completely mad.'

Soon after Clark's drinking session with Father Murphy, a message came in over the radio from São Gabriel da Cachoeira. The military were furious. Clark and the others had, they said, entered Indian land 'illegally'. They ordered Clark and his companions to remain where they were until military helicopters could fly to Pari Cachoeira and take them back.

The local Tukano leaders were aghast. This was, they were sure, an excuse by the military to regain a foothold among the Tukano. Community elders talked deep into the night. If the military took the foreigners away, they worried, the army might take the opportunity to change the reality on the ground. It was the last thing that the Tukano needed. They already had the church, which wouldn't let them speak their own language.

Were the military to return, it could be the beginning of the end for any remaining traces of Tukano independence.

Next morning, the Tukano leaders gave Clark and his friends a choice. Either they could wait at Pari Cachoeira for the helicopters to come and take them away, or Tukano guides would take them secretly to a Tukano goldmine in the Serra do Traíra, on the Colombian border. There, the military would not be able to follow or find them. Clark and his friends chose the goldmine.

It was an arduous journey. The rivers could only take them so far, and they needed to carry all of their supplies with them. To make matters worse, Jon and Jan were carrying 300 kilograms of equipment. They also refused to eat the local food of fish and *farinha*. Everyone else was travelling light, but the Danes' camera equipment and heavy canned food meant that each member of the party had to carry a 30-kilogram backpack.

For three days, Clark, the three Danes and five Tukano guides hiked through dense, mountainous jungle. They fought off attacks by killer bees and waded, sometimes knee-deep, through thick red mud. Back in Pari Cachoeira, the helicopters arrived to find that Clark and his travelling party had again slipped from their grasp. Infuriated, the soldiers returned to São Gabriel empty-handed.

Finally, the travellers arrived at the goldmine. Gold rushes were sweeping across the Amazon. It was Brazil's version of California's gold rush in the mid-nineteenth century, a lawless time on Brazil's Wild West frontier. Gold had been discovered on Tukano land in 1983. As soon as the news had travelled downriver, *garimpeiros*—prospectors—swarmed across the

Serra do Traíra. With the governor of Amazonas, Gilberto Mestrinho, cheering them on, more than 2000 *garimpeiros* took over the mines. A Tukano militia did its best to expel the miners from Tukano land. But they lost more often than they won. 'The white *garimpeiros* don't have the least civility,' one Tukano spokesman said at the time, 'and show much savagery when they quarrel with the Indians.'

By 1985, just four years before Clark and his friends arrived, the Serra do Traíra was dangerously close to anarchy. Unconfirmed reports emerged that the *garimpeiros* had massacred 60 Tukano who had been trying to defend the mines. The Tukano were getting desperate, so much so that one Tukano faction chose to swallow a bitter pill. They signed a 'gentlemen's agreement' with Paranapanema, the mining company backed by the Brazilian military, and granted a mining concession to Paranapanema. In 1988, the year before Clark arrived in Pari Cachoeira, the Tukano handed over most of their weapons and destroyed their traditional coca crops. In return, the Tukano would receive a share of mining proceeds, training in technical mining techniques, recognition of Indian sovereignty over the land and heightened security. Government investment in health, education and transport infrastructure was also part of the deal.

The Brazilian authorities kept few of their promises. But the mining company's militia did drive out the *garimpeiros*. And, luckily for the Tukano, Paranapanema never mined their concession. For a time at least, the Tukano regained control over the mines. The mines were still theirs when Clark and the three Danes arrived in the Serra do Traíra at the tail end of 1989.

Atop a mountain, the Tukano goldmine was like an apparition in the forest to Clark and his companions. Unlike the exploitation that had emerged from the mines of Serra Pelada, which was in Pará state, south of Belém and was shown in harrowing images by Sebastião Salgado in the mid-1980s, the Tukano mine in the Serra do Traíra was the lifeblood of a community. Conditions were primitive, to be sure. Yet there was a certain egalitarianism at play at the mine. Every Tukano man was allowed to spend three months—no more—at the mine and then return with the proceeds to his family. Six metres below the summit, a rich vein of gold, extracted manually, ran through the rock. Two men working hard for a whole day could, on average, finish the day with 50 grams of gold.

The mine stood in the heart of indigenous lands that spanned Colombia and Brazil, lands that protected twelve different indigenous peoples. From the summit, forest stretched to the horizon, deep inside Colombia. At the foot of the mountain flowed the Rio Traíra that marked the boundary between the two countries. Tukano guards kept at bay any influx of outside prospectors. And, unlike in so many other goldmines across the Amazon, the Tukano prohibited the use of mercury at the mine. It wasn't a utopian world. White river-traders often took advantage of the remote location and charged exorbitant prices for everything from salted fish to rubber boots. But the system worked, and the mine belonged to the Tukano.

Clark and the Danes stayed at the mine for two weeks, filming, getting to know the miners, learning how things worked. While they were there, news reached the mine that the president, José Sarney, had signed over a large tract of land to the Tukano. It is something of a tradition that Brazilian presidents hand over vast areas of land to indigenous groups in their final days, as if they no longer fear the consequences of doing so. It was one of Sarney's final acts as president. On the last night of Clark's stay, the Tukano threw a big party for the visiting group. The next morning, they set off for the return hike to Pari Cachoeira.

Two days into the hike, they met a party of Tukano on their way to the mine, and everybody shared a crate of cachaça (a distilled liquor made from fermented sugar cane, and a main ingredient in caipirinhas). Over the course of a night, the party drank themselves into a stupor. Falk later told Clark that the Scotsman had, at one point, leaned out of his hammock and vomited into his own shoes.

The real problem came next morning. As they loaded up the luggage, one of their five Indian guides, still drunk, opened a backpack and shrieked in indignation. The Tukano guides knew they had been carrying heavy equipment for Jon and Jan—power sources the size of car batteries, and a generator with which to charge the equipment. But they now discovered they had also been carrying a large stash of canned food, toiletries and other personal items for the two Danish filmmakers. For nearly an hour, the Tukano tried to get at the two men to kill them for their treachery. Clark and Falk were all that stood between Jon and Jan and certain death. Clark later laughed as he retold the story of himself and Falk, two hungover Europeans, dancing around and trying to protect two city boys from a posse of furious Indians in one of the most isolated places on Earth. It was, however, 'a really unpleasant situation'. Clark—who could easily have been killed by a stray spear thrown by a drunken guide—remained convinced that had the Indians not been intoxicated, they would have killed Jon and Jan in an instant.

Tukano anger shadowed the party back to Pari Cachoeira and spread through the community. People were no longer trying to kill Jon and Jan. Yet the Tukano leaders, sharing the guides' not-unreasonable conviction that the Danish camera crew had taken their people for a ride, refused to help the team return back downriver to São Gabriel da Cachoeira. Clark and the Danes were stranded.

In the end, it took all of Clark's persuasive powers over many days to convince the Tukano to transport them back down the river. The Indians took them as far as São Gabriel. Then they turned around and returned upriver without so much as a goodbye. In São Gabriel, Clark and the others quickly boarded their boat and left before the military realised that they were there.

When they returned to the land of radios and international news, they learned that the Berlin Wall had fallen while they were away.

If the 1970s were about the roads that opened up the Amazon and the first wave of deforestation that followed, the 1980s were when the first consequences of those years came into play. The 1980s were a prelude to conflicts that would erupt across the Amazon. The 1980s were when the battlelines were drawn.

This was the decade when the existential threats to Brazil's indigenous peoples took on greater urgency. In this, the fates of the Tukano, the Waimiri-Atroari and the Yanomami, all in the northern Amazon, were typical. Goldmining booms seeped out across Indian land in earnest from 1986, bringing disease to indigenous peoples and mercury to their rivers. There were incursions by military forces and settlers who often worked in tandem to drive Indians from their land. Increasingly, skirmishes over hydroelectric dams—the Tucuruí Dam on the Tocantins River in 1984, the Balbina Dam on the Uatumã River in 1987—added to the struggle for the Amazon's resources.

From these battles arose a growing international awareness of the Amazon. Musician Sting launched his Rainforest Foundation Fund in 1989. However well this played to an international audience, the world's sudden interest in the Amazon provoked a backlash inside Brazil. For many, calls by outsiders to save the Amazon were seen as an assault upon Brazil's sovereignty and good name. As a result, it became suddenly dangerous to advocate for the Amazon, its people and its wildlife. In this, the murder of activist Chico Mendes in December 1988 was the precursor to a culture of fear and impunity that still plagues the Amazon and those who would save it.

Looking back now, Clark's experience among the Tukano, and what happened next, were the opening salvos in the coming war for the Amazon. The Tukano's story would become a cautionary tale, a snapshot of an Amazon on the verge of great change and even greater peril.

~

Clark returned to Manaus, then home to Italy. He hadn't been home for long when he received a phone call from two Tukano leaders, Pedro and Dominique Machado. Brazil's army had invaded the Serra do Traíra mine, driven the Tukano on a forced march into the forest and destroyed the Tukano settlement in the mountains.

A second-hand account of what happened survives, told to Alcida Rita Ramos by Tukano sources:

> On 9 May 1990, 123 Tukano men, women and children were expelled from their land in the upper Uaupés region by twenty-eight soldiers of the Brazilian army . . . Claiming the Indians were involved in gold smuggling and, as an extension, with drug traffic and Colombian guerrillas, the soldiers forced the Indians out of their homes at gunpoint and made them walk for days along heavily flooded paths carrying all their belongings to the villages of relatives . . . To crown the expulsion, the army men burnt the Indian houses and destroyed their gold panning equipment.

The Machados told Clark that the army had dropped incendiary bombs and machine-gunned the Tukano canoes and encampments. Miraculously, only one Tukano person was killed.

Clark called Fiona Watson at Survival International in London. The NGO quickly launched an investigation, confirmed that the stories were true and began an urgent international campaign to bring the Brazilian army to account. Through the Danish NGO Nepenthes, Clark raised funds for

Miguel Barrella—a Brazilian lawyer, based in Manaus, who would later become Clark's friend and collaborator, to visit the mine on a fact-finding mission. There Barrella confirmed the details of the army attack. He even photographed unexploded munitions that the army had dropped from helicopters at the site.

Tukano leaders took their case to the capital, Brasília. Brazilian NGOs, supposedly set up to advocate for indigenous causes, did nothing to help. Eventually, the Tukano leaders found their way to Brazil's army minister, attorney-general and senator Romeu Tuma. Tuma was the former director of the federal police and the man to whom the Tukano had personally handed over their guns a few years earlier.

The persistence of the Tukano's representatives in Brasília, Survival International's campaign and the evidence gathered by Barrella paid off. It was a public relations disaster for Brazil's embarrassed civilian government. Here was another lesson of the 1980s: that the world cared about the Amazon and could, through their pressure and by casting the spotlight upon remote corners of the rainforest, curb the worst excesses of those who would destroy the forest and its peoples.

Although by no means the final word in the Tukano's war for survival and independence, it was an important victory. 'The army eventually ended up paying out something like 2000 kilograms of gold in compensation to the Tukano Indians for what they did,' Clark later recalled. Indigenous communities across the Amazon basin celebrated.

Clark may not have seen it this way at the time, but the whole episode offered him his first taste of advocating for the

Amazon and its people. He was, it turned out, rather good at it. This was just as well. The next time he returned to the Amazon, later in 1990, he would be given a far greater mission, one that he would spend the rest of his life trying to fulfil.

# 10

# The Challenge

*1990–1992*

By 1990, Clark was a regular visitor to Brazil. Drawn to the rivers of the Amazon basin and to the communities that lived along their shores, he travelled extensively with a changeable but tight cast of friends.

Erik Falk, who had accompanied Clark on his adventure into the lands of the Tukano, was always there. Six years after they first met in a bar in Belém in 1984, Falk and Clark were firm friends. Falk was nearly fifteen years older than Clark. He was a formidable character and a reassuring presence on their journeys into the Amazon, having honed his survival skills as a member of Denmark's elite Jaeger Corps, a special operations unit with notoriously exacting entry requirements. Only 10 per cent of applicants pass tests that include cold-water combat in icy waters, twelve-hour marches with heavy packs, and withstanding mental disintegration.

Daniel Garibotti, an Argentinian whom Clark had collected along the way and who would be his friend for many years, often came along. Plinho Encarnação was also a regular, as was João, another local friend. Plinho and João were local touchstones for Clark. They provided contacts and wisdom, and they confirmed that Clark had no intention of keeping Brazil at arm's length. Were Clark to make Brazil home, it would be full immersion spent not among expats but among Brazilians. When they travelled the Rio Negro, Valdemar—Clark's wise, marijuana-growing indigenous friend—was with them as well. Valdemar was a reminder, if any was needed, that Clark's future lay among the true inhabitants of the forest.

Clark and whoever was to accompany him would meet in Manaus. There they hung out with locals and drank together in the bars where they planned their next adventure. Manaus was a means to an end and its appeal quickly wore thin. Once they had decided where they were going, they would set out quickly, forsaking as soon as they could the main channels of the river, slowing down once they reached the lesser-known tributaries where the forest was dense and people were scarce.

Over time their focus narrowed. They spent more and more time exploring the Rio Negro, which was quieter and more remote than the Amazon east of Manaus. Dense forests lined the banks of the Negro's tributaries. The Rio Negro had far fewer mosquitoes than other rivers. And, besides, the Rio Jauaperi was Valdemar's home territory. Since Clark first met Valdemar at the mouth of the Jauaperi in 1984, the two men had formed a deep bond. Clark loved the river, yes, but he also loved the time he spent with Valdemar. Unlike Clark's other friends, Valdemar rarely strayed far from home.

In 2018, during my visit to Xixuaú, when Clark and Valdemar had been friends for more than 30 years, Clark spoke with rare emotion about their first meeting. 'I fell in love with Valdemar the very first time I met him, and we've been very good friends ever since. He's one of these men in the world that are a focal point for me.' The others he identified as Falk; his father, Colin; and Oliviero, the father of Anna Bonari. 'Most of the important men in my life have died, so he's one of the few who is left. Valdemar is a rock. He's been there for a long time. He's a rock in my life, and most of the other rocks in my life have gone.'

Clark and Valdemar were easy friends. I often found them sitting by the riverbank, facing the water and deep in easy conversation. Each listened carefully to the other, and their conversations meandered, as without haste as the rivers that passed by and that they journeyed along. When there was nothing to say, neither felt any need to fill the silence. Clark made Valdemar tell his story over and again, perhaps seeing in it some key to understanding this land that he loved.

Six years older than Clark, Valdemar was born in 1954 on the Camanaú River, not far east of Xixuaú. Like the Jauaperi, the Camanaú flows down into the Rio Negro through the lands of the Waimiri-Atroari. Valdemar belonged to the Baniwa, an indigenous people whose lands once extended throughout north-western Brazil and into Colombia and Venezuela. The Baniwa paid the price for never straying far from accessible major rivers. Slavers had always found them easily and then, in the twentieth century, non-indigenous settlers further eroded Baniwa numbers and independence.

Valdemar lived a true forest life. He was the youngest of nine children: seven sisters survived; his only brother died of malaria. His parents lived entirely from the forest, working as itinerant rubber-tappers for four months of the year, then fishing, hunting and harvesting Brazil nuts for the remainder. Valdemar never went to school and worked alongside his parents almost from the age when he could walk. When Valdemar was ten, his father died. Two, perhaps three years later, his mother, too, passed away.

In the years before he met Clark, Valdemar worked all across the region. He was a fisherman, a feller of timber, and a harvester of rubber and Brazil nuts just like his parents before him. He even worked for a time hunting and skinning the giant otters and beautiful cats—margays, ocelots, oncillas and, yes, jaguars—of the forest. In the service of the fur trade, Valdemar would help to kill 20 or 30 cats in a two-week expedition. The forest at that time was a place of plenty. In an area where now there are perhaps 10,000 people spread across a number of villages and thousands of square kilometres, back then there were, Valdemar remembered, just three houses.

These were perhaps odd pursuits for a man who would later become Clark's staunchest companion in the struggle to save the rainforest. But at the time, such a life was all that there was for someone like Valdemar. And as he later said, 'I was young in those days. I never thought about it.' As he ranged across the region, traversing Xixuaú and beyond, he came to know the barely discernible trails and quiet backwaters of this corner of the Amazon better than almost anyone alive.

Valdemar may have had no experience in conservation. But when it came to the forest, he possessed what Brazilians call *jeito*. The word means 'way' in Portuguese, but has come to mean a certain savvy or, in the Amazon, forest smarts. Valdemar had never gone to school but he knew the forest, and he was uniquely placed to notice the changes that were occurring. Where once Valdemar and his companions had the area to themselves, there were more hunters arriving with each passing year. The cats and otters were becoming harder to find.

Before Clark arrived in 1984, Valdemar had married and had children, and had begun a more sedentary lifestyle at the mouth of the Jauaperi. In the six years to 1990, Clark and Valdemar met every year.

By then Anna Bonari was pregnant and important decisions were looming for her and Clark, just as they were for Valdemar. Clark knew that it was time to do more than just travel, and with a new family on the way, his carefree life would no longer be so simple.

The Amazon at the time was—and to a certain extent remains—Brazil's Wild West, where a handful of colonising families eked out subsistence lives in vast territories. They built lonely homesteads, each one a stake planted in the wilderness, each a pioneer's leap into the unknown. These homesteads were courageous, yet desperate and forlorn. They were acts of individual survival as much as they were first steps on behalf of an entire civilisation. The pioneers, the homesteaders, opened up the wilderness. It was piecemeal at first. But each one made possible what would follow. Not all would survive. Of those who did, their offspring or subsequent generations would often, after the West was won and the wilderness gone, make the reverse journey. Where the pioneers saw opportunity, their children and grandchildren saw only obscurity and backwardness. They would flee to the cities, the new frontiers of opportunity for the rural poor. There they would find squalor and slums and a world as alien and as frightening to them as the forests had been to the first settlers. All of that would come later.

For now, these rivers and forests remained wild and lawless places where outposts were few. The Amazon was where people came to seek their fortunes and to leave their pasts behind. Some came to attempt to tame the wilderness. Genocide of indigenous peoples often followed. The frontier was a blank canvas for those wanting to write new myths and new stories that might change the course of history—their own or the nation's. It is the enduring call of the frontier. The frontier changes men and women. It drives them crazy and pushes them to pursue riches and lives from which there is no return. Clark's intentions were unclear, but he understood the impulse. He, too, saw salvation in the forest far removed from his old life, beyond where the last paved road ended.

These romantic notions of the frontier were, for Valdemar, as mystifying as the world that lay beyond the rivers and forests. By 1990, he was considering moving in the opposite direction, to the city, so that his children could go to school. Valdemar himself could not read or write. But he was wise enough to know that the modern world was coming, and he wanted his kids to be ready.

So it was that these two close friends, Clark, 30, and Valdemar, 36, spoke of the future as they drifted, each time further north up the Jauaperi River.

On one river journey in 1990, Clark returned to the Jauaperi. It was his fifth trip on the river and with him were, among others, his brother Paul, Plinho, Erik, and Tom Haycraft, a family friend of the Clarks. 'It was March and the water level in the river was rising,' Clark later wrote. 'We went further up than I had ever been before and came to the mouth of a small tributary. There was a beautiful golden sandbank at the confluence of the two rivers. The beach was an excellent place to tie up the boat. The side river turned out to be the most enchanting place I had ever visited here in the Amazon. The water was extraordinarily clear and the fish were abundant to the point of being ridiculous.'

Clark and his friends had stumbled on Xixuaú. Clark was spellbound. Giant otters came to investigate their arrival, and an anaconda swam alongside their canoe. The pink river dolphins that I would see at Xixuaú nearly three decades later were everywhere. No other boats passed by while they were there. They heard no engine noise other than that of their own boat. There were more manatees, monkeys and macaws than there were people. It was the time of low water, and broad sandy beaches separated river from forest. When entering the water to bathe or swim, they had to be careful not to step on stingrays.

To the north lay the lands of the Waimiri-Atroari. South of Xixuaú, the Jauaperi's deserted shore ran for hours of slow river travel in an unbroken line of forest on both sides of the river. Clark and his companions felt something akin to euphoria as they enjoyed campfires on the beaches, and drifted without destination through the channels and byways of the *igarapés* of Xixuaú. It felt like paradise.

When they finally had to leave, on their way back down-river they pulled into the small village of São Pedro. São Pedro clung to the banks of the Rio Jauaperi, north of the Rio Negro. Like some doomed outpost on the furthermost reaches of the known world, it was a brave little place with its back to the forest and its face to the river. Then, as now, São Pedro was little more than a scattering of wooden plank houses built on the stilts that protect homes from the annual rising of the waters. The yearly floods here cause water levels to rise ten to 15 metres, expanding the river's girth up the shoreline and into the forest. When water levels were low in São Pedro, the Jauaperi was barely 300 metres across, and the riverbank was bare earth. Colossal trees and tangled palms dwarfed the houses. Beyond that, most of São Pedro, such as it was, remained invisible behind the wall of trees.

Aside from an isolated house or two, São Pedro did not exist when Valdemar was a boy. There was, however, a community of sorts: a family here, another not far away. An itinerant population of people also came and went as they used the river and surrounding forest to make a living, much as Valdemar and his family had done for most of their lives.

Clark had been to São Pedro before and knew those who

lived here. He also knew some of those who passed through on their way to essential business in the forest or on the river. He liked the Jauaperi, and not only because Valdemar lived nearby. On his journeys throughout the Amazon basin, Clark had seen where lone *fazendas* (farms or ranch houses) had become villages, and where villages had become towns. This growing human presence had come to define the modern Amazon. Clark had seen their march even in the six years that he had been travelling up the river. Everywhere, the balance was shifting, humankind replacing the forest as the Amazon's dominant force, shrinking the tree cover as human settlements extended along the riverbank and into the interior. But up here, north of the Rio Negro, things were different. Up the Jauaperi, the forest remained relatively intact. People were few. Clark felt free here. And now he had fallen for the region upriver called Xixuaú.

When Clark and his companions landed in São Pedro in 1990, elders from the village and from neighbouring communities were waiting for them. 'We are poor,' they told him. 'We have no schools for our children, no health service when we are sick, no way to make a living except killing animals. A lot of the families are moving to the slums of Manaus or Novo Airão or Barcelos. We don't want to leave here. We like this place, but it's impossible to live here. You come here every year. We know you and we know you like our river. Why don't you help us, so we don't have to abandon our homes and move to the city?'

In this, São Pedro was every small and remote community in the Amazon. Young people—Indians and *caboclos*—were streaming into the slums of Manaus and Belém, and as far afield as São Paulo and Rio de Janeiro. There they sought their fortunes and their escape from the obscurity of rural life. It was one of the great ironies of the modern Amazon: remote communities were dying even as roads and a thirst for the Amazon's resources brought human settlements ever deeper into once-remote regions of the forest.

With the outside world beaming into even one-television towns, young people saw a world beyond, a world where people their own age drove fancy cars, wore nice clothes and otherwise had access to a whole world of possibility. Twelve-hour, even sixteen-hour days spent fishing or tapping rubber just to feed their families, coupled with the ennui of riverbank life, may have sustained their parents. But it simply wasn't enough to keep young people in the villages. With the old ways disappearing, there was nothing for them here.

Far from the nearest road and accessible only by river, São Pedro was increasingly home only to the very old and the very young. Confronted with São Pedro's cry for help, Clark understood the problem immediately.

Clark also knew straightaway the magnitude of what he was being asked to do. It was the kind of problem that confounded policy experts from the World Bank and governments the world over. Untold billions of dollars had been thrown at the problem. Some of the best and brightest minds in NGOs and UN agencies had grappled with the issue, turning rural communities in developing nations into an industry. Few of the initiatives had succeeded in stemming the slow and inexorable emptying of rural communities, probably forever.

Clark and the others stayed in São Pedro for a few days. All the while, they discussed the challenge they had been presented with. Back and forth they went, arguing among themselves and talking it over with the elders. They drank a lot, cachaça mostly, and for a time they felt defeated by the enormity of the task. Clark remembered thinking at the time, 'What do I do? Go back to Europe and say "Anybody want to help a bunch of poor people in Brazil in the Amazon?" That's not very sexy.'

At the end of the second day, Clark had a lightbulb moment. Whether it was his idea alone or it emerged from the haze of sometimes drunken conversation, no one can remember. In Clark's telling 28 years later, he went to the elders and said, 'Maybe we can do something. What if we set up a protected area?'

The elders seemed to like the idea. Clark knew just the place.

There had been a village at Xixuaú until the 1950s. As so often happens out here, a village elder, in this case Teodorico Nascimento, died and the community fell apart. The only house Clark and the others had found in Xixuaú belonged to a *caboclo* family who were the direct descendants of Nascimento. When Clark had first arrived, the patriarch, Carlos Alberto Nascimento—Carlito—was unloading a boat full of booze. He was drunk most of the time they were there. Later, he admitted that he hoarded the colourful rubbish that surrounded his hut so as to make his home more beautiful. There was a small clearing, a small plot for growing manioc, and that was it. It was a true frontier homestead, a tiny scar in the forest.

It was not enough for Clark just to fall in love with Xixuaú. He wanted to save it. The more they talked, the more the idea of a nature reserve appealed to Clark and his friends, both for its own sake and as a way to help local people like Carlito. Clark had found his place. But he still didn't quite know what to make of it.

Clark knew enough about how the Amazon worked to know that although Carlito and his lonely family were the only permanent inhabitants for miles around, others came and went. In season, they gathered Brazil nuts from the surrounding forest. At other times, they tapped rubber. Year-round, they fished and hunted and generally took from the forest what they needed. Then they moved on.

Land ownership out here on the frontier existed in the shadow of the law. If it belonged to anyone, it belonged to the government. It was public land. That didn't mean that the government controlled this land. It was, in fact, unlikely that any government official had ever done anything more than pass by in a boat this far upriver. Xixuaú was what's called *terra devoluta*, or unclaimed public land. To this day, the words *terra devoluta* appear on maps representing the Amazon's uninhabited tracts. The way it always worked in the Amazon was that those who set up a home in the wilderness acquired some form of squatters' rights to the land. They became the *posseiros*, the possessors of the land. It wasn't theirs. They weren't the owners. Nor did they get a title, at least not at first. What they did get under the law, if not on paper, were the rights to live on and use the land.

Those rights were even enforceable. Under an old law known as the *direito de posse*, the squatters or *posseiros* were entitled to compensation if ever they were evicted. Codified in Article 502 of Brazil's old Civil Code, this law also allowed *posseiros* to use all necessary force to defend their land.

In the old days in America's Wild West, anyone who didn't mind the danger and the isolation could seek out an empty place and plant a stake. They became stakeholders. It was the same in the Amazon. The arrangement suited everyone—except, of course, the indigenous peoples whose lands they were on, and whose connection to the land should have been inviolable. Governments had neither the resources nor the inclination to police these places so far removed from urban areas. And, anyway, having someone else clear the forest and open up the way to those who would follow suited the government's needs. The arrangement suited frontiersmen and women, too. Independent-minded and often on the run from past lives and indiscretions, they wanted nothing to do with the authorities. A land without an owner meant, in theory, that you could find a stretch of uninhabited land, build a little hut and plant your little plantation, safe in the knowledge that if no one with a prior claim turned up, it was effectively yours.

But it was rarely that simple. Land rights in the Amazon are a tangle of competing interests. Indigenous peoples, ranchers and homesteaders all make claims of ownership. Rubber-tappers, Brazil-nut harvesters, fisherfolk and hunters all claim right of access. In this context, and in the absence of any meaningful government authority out in the backblocks, actual rights are very often less important than the ability to enforce one's claims, usually through violence. On such occasions, someone almost always ends up getting hurt. What one Brazilian government minister said in 1973 remains true: 'The Amazon is still in the bandit stage. It is only later that the sheriff will be required.'

Back in the early 1990s when Clark and his companions were considering setting something up in Xixuaú, they were fortunate. Xixuaú was as far as you could go up the Jauaperi without hitting Waimiri-Atroari land. No one wanted to mess with the Indians and no one wanted them as neighbours. It was also too far from Manaus and the Rio Negro to be economically viable; there were easier pickings elsewhere. No one else was interested.

Clark talked with his friends. He spent time speaking with the few people he met anywhere on the river. He also consulted Miguel Barrella, the Manaus lawyer who had worked with Clark to investigate the military attacks on the Tukano. Together they came up with a plan that, according to Clark, had never been tried before. In 1992, they formed an association, with one chapter based in Brazil and the other in Italy. As a legal entity, the association provided the legal framework for fundraising. It also provided a legal foundation for creating the reserve that Clark hoped would save the forest and the local communities of the Jauaperi.

It wasn't Clark's association, although he was a member. In their conversations, Clark and Barrella discussed the people who had spent part of their lives living and working up and down the river. It was to be their association. If they sold their rights—to the land, to access the land—to the association, the association would hold the land in common. The people who signed over their rights would get paid for doing so, even as they retained their rights to use the land. It was a pretty good deal.

In 1990, the Brazilian government had decreed the first of what were called extractive reserves, which were protected areas where locals were allowed to use or 'extract' subsistence resources. Still one of the largest protected areas in the Brazilian Amazon, the Reserva Extrativista Chico Mendes (Chico Mendes Extractive Reserve) came into being in the state of Acre, in the Amazon's south. It was named after Chico Mendes, the famous rubber-tapper turned activist who was murdered in 1988. Mendes had understood that some areas of the rainforest could be protected only if the rights of those who sought subsistence in the forest were part of the equation. It provided a model for what Clark hoped would happen in Xixuaú in the future. Until then, the association would hold onto the land and protect it.

Clark and Barrella began piecing together the complicated web of historical rights and obligations, deciding who had sufficient connection to the land to become a part of the association. Carlito and his family were the only ones living at Xixuaú. But they had to take into account, in Clark's words, 'some of the older people on the river who had, at one time, when they were young, lived here, or other people who still came here every year to harvest the Brazil nuts in a certain area'. As much as the idea borrowed from the philosophical framework that underpinned the extractive reserves, the association was a clever use of the chaos that ruled out on the frontier.

Yes, the idea of paying them to join an association with rights over the land rewarded them for having opened up the land to exploitation. But now that they were there, by signing on they forfeited nothing except any exclusive claim to rights over the land. Clark and the association were offering them money for something (the right to access and use the land) they already had but that had never been codified. They would still be able to use the land for their own subsistence needs. In return, Clark and the association would be able to build a sense of community with shared rights and responsibilities to care for the land.

Their plan didn't always have the desired effect. Some used the money to make the very journey that the elders of São Pedro had been desperate to stop. Suddenly flush with money, Carlito's wife left Xixuaú and bought herself a house in Manaus. And it wasn't always easy. The fledgling association had no money and Clark made the first payments out of his own pocket.

But, in time, the association and its members controlled nearly 70,000 hectares (700 square kilometres) of land, centred on Xixuaú and north towards the Xiparina. A wealthy Italian prince who was a friend of Chris's donated US$100,000 (A$135,000) to pay for a Brazilian topography company to demarcate the reserve's boundary. To do this, they planted markers every 200 metres around the reserve's border.

As word spread, people from neighbouring communities came forward, hoping to join. Clark realised that the association needed money, both for purchasing the rights to Xixuaú, but also as a means for the locals to make money going forward. If they saw ongoing benefits from the association and the reserve, so the argument ran, then they would remain invested in its success. Clark's Argentinian friend Daniel Garibotti had a large collection of Amazonian handicrafts, and he, Clark, and Tom Haycraft sold these in Europe to raise funds. As a longer-term source of income for the association and its running costs, Clark also began advertising tourist expeditions to the Amazon.

The elders of São Pedro were thrilled. Locals were excited at the prospect of making money. The reserve even had a marked perimeter. The protection of Xixuaú was underway.

Clark and his friends sat back and waited for the backlash to begin.

# 11

# Threats

*1992–2000*

Clark was spending more and more time in the Amazon. Unlike in earlier years when he and his friends ranged far and wide, they now swapped exploration for something more substantive. They had a project. His friends joined him when they could. Anna Bonari was a constant presence on these trips. So, too, was their daughter, Cathleen, who had been born in Grosseto, Italy, in October 1990. Clark was a doting father. Not long after Cathleen was born, he began work on a story he hoped one day to publish but never did. I have seen it. It was the story of Clark's journey to Xixuaú and the broader story of the Amazon. It's called 'The Amazon Sunset'.

I first met Clark as an older man, when he was 57. By then he was world-weary and calm. He smiled easily, and he'd lost none of his idealism. But life had taught him to be guarded. Those who knew him in the early 1990s—when he was in his early thirties—describe his tremendous capacity for joy. He was a dreamer, a single-minded man driven by crazy ideas and by passions, some would say obsessions. One of those was his family. The other was Xixuaú and all that it meant. Little else mattered. Fortunately for Clark, Bonari, for the most part, shared Clark's passions. When Cathleen was just three months old, in early 1991, they took her to Brazil and far up the Amazon. People thought they were crazy.

They continued to travel often back and forth between Brazil and Italy. When they were in Brazil, they spent as much time as they could in Xixuaú. They talked with the community. They signed people up to the association. And they began to build their home by the lagoon at Xixuaú, surrounded by the forest.

Carlito lived where the whole village had stood back in the 1950s. Across the water, Clark and his friends built a lovely, large *maloca*, one of the big communal spaces with a soaring roof that is a feature of so many Amazonian communities. At the beginning, everyone slept in hammocks and in simple huts arrayed along the riverbank. Friends and family and tourists came and went, and slowly a community grew. Most of Clark's and his family's visits lasted no longer than three months at a time, which was all that their Brazilian visas allowed. When forced to leave, they'd return to Italy. There Clark would dabble in Tuscan home restoration or they'd work in odd jobs to raise money for their return. Fundraising for projects at Xixuaú and organising tourist visits took up much of their time. It was a natural progression. Xixuaú had very quickly become their life. Everything else they did focused on pursuing that dream, so much so that when Bonari realised she was pregnant in Italy in 1993, they hurriedly packed their bags and flew to Manaus, where Nicolle was born later that year. It was a statement of intent. Brazil was now home. They also knew that having a child born on Brazilian soil could prove invaluable when it came to getting permanent residency.

Clark's older brother Paul was a frequent visitor and collaborator. After his first trip in 1984, he returned with his Italian wife, Bianca, in 1990, and again in 1992. Paul was at something of a loose end in Italy. None too thrilled with Silvio Berlusconi's emergence as a political force, he and Bianca were looking for a fresh challenge. Sometime near the end of 1993, or early 1994, Chris came to Paul with an offer. Tourists were starting to trickle in and the Xixuaú community was growing. Paul had been among those who helped to build the *maloca*. He knew many of the people there. Many of them, perhaps as many as 90 per cent of the adults, were illiterate. Chris Clark wanted Paul and Bianca to move to Xixuaú, as caretakers and schoolteachers. They agreed.

At the same time, Valdemar was living at Xixuaú. Valdemar loved the whole idea of what was happening there. Whenever Clark was there, he and Valdemar were inseparable. But Valdemar was conflicted. He was happy enough with his own life. Deep down, though, Valdemar had always felt that his children would need a formal education if they were to make their way in the world. For all his passion for Xixuaú, Valdemar was still planning on moving to Novo Airão so that his children could go to school. He told Clark that he would only stay if his children could get an education. There were many reasons for building a school at Xixuaú. Keeping Valdemar in the community was one of them.

The school began at Xixuaú with, as Paul later described it to me, 'a stick in the sand'. Over time, they built a school, one that remains at Xixuaú to this day.

But as time went on, cracks began to appear in the relationship between Chris and Paul. Both were passionate about the Amazon. They shared a vision for a nature reserve that protected the river and the forest. And Paul agreed with his younger brother that the communities of the Jauaperi had to benefit from the reserve. But where Chris argued that a regular flow of tourists was essential to the success of Xixuaú, by providing funds for projects and a steady income for locals, Paul worried that the growing community ran counter to the very idea of protecting the finite resources of the local environment. On the one hand, Chris and his friends took every opportunity to sign up as many local people as possible to the association; they were, they argued, paying people for something they didn't even know they owned. On the other, Paul felt uncomfortable with the idea that locals who were unable to read or write were signing important documents while he and Bianca were teaching the kids of these same people how to read.

The brothers also argued over strategy and the role played by the local authorities. Paul felt that a collaborative approach was best. *We've got nothing to hide*, he argued. He wanted to be up-front from the beginning. *Get the local authorities on board*, he said, *and they'll get behind the project.*

*Rubbish*, Chris would reply. *They're not going to allow a bunch of foreigners to come in and set up a nature reserve. We're*

*not making any money here. We're doing it for the local commu-*
*nity. The authorities would twist their motives, Chris argued.*
*They might even try to stir up the locals against the project. If*
*that happened, there would be no going back. The authorities*
*might even try to take over. Far better to fly under the radar.*

Following this rationale, they signed the association's
founding papers at a private notary's office without ceremony.
Then they set about laying the groundwork for the reserve on
the ground and hoped that no one would notice. By the time
they did, Clark hoped, momentum towards a reserve would be
unstoppable.

Paul felt that Chris should have been more diplomatic.
Chris was convinced that his brother was being naïve about
the intentions of Brazilian politicians.

Both were right. Soon enough the tensions would come to
a head.

Not everyone was thrilled with what Chris Clark was doing.

In 1992, Rio de Janeiro hosted the United Nations Conference
on Environment and Development (UNCED), known as the
Earth Summit. The world's attention was on Brazil. Whether
or not the Brazilian government of then-president Fernando
Collor de Mello shared the world's concern about threats to
the Amazon, it was a public relations coup for the country on
the international stage. Deforestation had been gathering pace
for more than a decade. Documentaries by Adrian Cowell (*The
Decade of Destruction*), and the publicity generated by Sting

and others, had turned the Amazon into an international concern. The 1992 Earth Summit was the forerunner to the Paris Agreement and the Kyoto Protocol. Some 150 world leaders signed agreements. Under one of these statements the leaders issued, governments pledged 'not to carry out any activities on the lands of indigenous peoples that would cause environmental degradation or that would be culturally inappropriate'. It felt like real change on a global scale might be just around the corner. Deforestation even slowed in the summit's aftermath.

If to the rest of the world it looked like a watershed moment for the Amazon, it all played out very differently inside Brazil. Many Brazilians resented outsiders telling them what to do with their forest. It didn't help when, three years prior to Earth Summit, US Republican senator Bob Kasten, of Wisconsin, had said on 3 January 1989, 'The fact is, we need them and we use them—so they're our rain forests too.' Politicians and conservative commentators warned that the international agreements were a front. The high-minded press releases and policy promises weren't about the environment, they said. They were, instead, a naked power grab by a world hungry for Brazil's natural resources. The world, they said, wanted to turn the Amazon into a 'green Persian Gulf'. For all the goodwill at Rio in 1992, Brazil's foreign minister showed that he also understood his domestic audience when he said, 'Brazil will not see itself turned into a botanical garden for the rest of humanity.'

Clark had already had a taste of what that could mean. In 1984, a disgruntled local had fired shots at the boat of Clark's friend, Miguel, when they tried to protect local turtles on the Amazon. A few years later, a Manaus landowner had hired someone to burn down the place Clark and his friends were staying in the forest. At Xixuaú, Clark was not just signing up locals to their association. He was also going up against those whose activities ran contrary to the goals of any reserve. 'We'd go after anybody who was putting out a fishing net, or cutting down a tree or whatever,' Clark told me. This rarely went down well. 'This was getting so many people against us that there was even a risk that we would be killed.'

In 1996, Clark was at Xixuaú when a local politician named Francisco da Silva (not his real name) turned up. Clark was there with his friend Paolo Roberto. Roberto and Clark were working on a malaria-eradication project in the Jauaperi region. Roberto was quite the glamorous friend. He belonged, Clark said, to 'one of the families in Italy who can be traced back 2000 years to the noble book, to the Roman Empire. He's the Prince of Puglia and the Two Sicilies, and I don't know what.' It was Roberto who had paid for the demarcation of the reserve's boundaries. He also helped to fund an expansion of the association by bringing the Xiparina River and its people into what they hoped would be the reserve. Francisco may have been the area's local member in the Roraima state parliament, but locals had no idea who he was. They'd never seen him before. An election was looming and Francisco had come to solicit votes and donations.

Francisco arrived at Clark's *maloca* in his motorboat. As Clark remembered it, Francisco walked up the stairs and said, 'You guys are rich!'

Clark welcomed him. He explained to the politician what they were doing at Xixuaú. He told the politician how all of their money was going into the reserve. Right now, they explained, their focus was ensuring that Francisco's constituents weren't dying from malaria. Perhaps, as the local member, he might like to help? 'Francisco says to us, "I could be very useful for you guys, for what you're trying to do here. But I would need a donation for my election campaign."' Clark shook his head as he told me this: 'A typical Brazilian politician.' Clark and Roberto politely demurred.

Then the nightmare began.

Francisco wasn't used to people saying no, and his revenge was swift and wide-reaching. At first, he tapped into the zeitgeist of the times by denouncing Clark and Xixuaú as part of a foreign invasion of the area. 'We began to hear rumours that a story was going around regarding the foreigners in the Xixuaú who had illegally taken over a huge area of land, larger than Denmark, enslaved the local people, closed off entire rivers with chains and padlocks, and opened up areas of the forest to grow marijuana.' Francisco launched legal challenges to the legality of the association. He also became the driving force behind a series of parliamentary inquiries—one at a municipal level, one in the state parliament, and two in Brazil's federal parliament—that investigated Clark and tried to shut down Xixuaú.

Clark's failure to contribute to Francisco's re-election was clearly a personal affront to the politician. Why else would he take the considerable effort of travelling deep into the jungle, far from the comforts of the state capital, to personally threaten Clark and his family? Once, when Chris Clark was away, Francisco arrived at Xixuaú. Paul Clark was there with his wife Bianca. 'Francisco arrived with *heavily* armed military policemen,' Paul would later tell me. 'He stormed up the wooden steps, into the tiny *maloca*. Bianca and I had no idea who he was or what he wanted. We had a straw roof and he took his lighter out and just started flicking the flame near the straw, saying, "We're gonna burn you out. We're gonna throw you into the middle of the river."' Francisco made it clear the Clarks' crime was being foreigners.

The visitors in uniform kept on coming.

Clark's address book wasn't restricted to Italian princes. He had struck up a friendship with Lady Madeleine Kleinwort, a British heiress from the Kleinwort Benson bank of Geneva. Over the years that they were involved at Xixuaú, Lady Kleinwort, through the Ernest Kleinwort Charitable Trust, funded solar power and a satellite internet connection for the village through the US-based Solar Electric Light Fund. Lady Kleinwort's daughter, Selina, spent three months of her gap year in 2000 living at Xixuaú, helping out in the various projects and teaching English to the children of local families. At the end of the three months, Lady Kleinwort flew to Xixuaú in a seaplane to pick up her daughter, and to spend time seeing Xixuaú for herself.

Early one morning, while Lady Kleinwort was enjoying one of those gloriously peaceful Xixuaú dawns, two big outboards stormed into Xixuaú and pulled up at the landing to Clark's *maloca*. Men in full military fatigues, armed with machine guns and wearing balaclavas, careered up the steps. It was a serious mission. They trained their guns on everyone at the *maloca*. Among the party were army soldiers, military police and civilian police, and there were too many of them to count. Clark heard the commotion and came out to greet them. He recalled how the head of the mission, a Japanese-Brazilian police delegate from São Paulo named Oscar Kyoto, demanded to know where the laboratory was. Clark was mystified. 'The laboratory? You don't mean the lavatory?'

Lady Kleinwort remembered it as quite the adventure. It was like being in a movie, she told me when I tracked her down in Argentina in 2020. She was warm and gracious during our conversation and I could almost hear her shaking her head in disbelief down the phone line. 'I have a very vivid impression of it, not of details, but of watching these big boats, bristling with soldiers and guns and things. It was very aggressive.'

As always when recounting such events, Clark laughed as he told me what happened next. I imagined him trying not to laugh as Brazil's version of the Wild West posse arrived, convinced that they were hot on the trail of dangerous outlaws. Kyoto and his men began interrogating the local people. What were these foreigners doing here? There was only one problem: the police from São Paulo couldn't understand the Portuguese spoken by these rural Amazonian *caboclos*, and the problem was mutual. In the end, Clark ended up being both the accused and the translator. Kyoto could make out just enough to know that Clark was faithfully interpreting what the locals were saying. They conducted exhaustive searches of Clark's meagre possessions. And they soon learned that what they had been told was going on at Xixuaú bore little resemblance to what was happening on the ground. The locals were happy. They didn't feel exploited. They defended Clark, and told Kyoto that Clark had brought great benefits to the area and that they wanted him to stay. The locals had just caught two giant *tucunaré* (peacock bass). Would they like to stay for dinner? Kyoto and his men stayed for a couple of days. Having found nothing, they left, but not before Oscar Kyoto had the good grace to pull Clark aside and tell him, 'If I lived here, I'd be a part of this association too.'

Such visits became a part of life at Xixuaú. Anna Bonari remembered how the pattern was always the same. 'They came with balaclavas and with guns. They had everything. They came very angry. We knew they were coming because the boys heard motors from long, long away on the river. As soon as they arrived, we were there waiting for them. They always ended the same way: after two hours, we would all be sitting at the table having a coffee. Everybody had calmed down, because they saw the real situation. We had this so many times in our lives.'

Even when episodes like this ended well, the constant threats were very real. Threats to kill were common in the Amazon. No sphere of Amazonian life was exempt. They lurked unspoken in the dark corners of political deal-making as a reminder of where power lay. Often more overt in the world of business where bodyguards doubled as hitmen, threats and their consequences were simply part of the cost of doing business. But there was no more dangerous place to be in the Amazon than in a dispute over land.

As always on the frontier, land was at the centre of everything. It was where the line between business and politics was at its most murky. Wealthy local landowners were very often powerful local politicians. Landless peasants were seen as expendable, but they were also increasingly close to uprising. Those who advocated on their behalf were considered a danger to the established order. Out in the provinces, legal checks and balances that kept politician-businesspeople from exercising excessive power were meaningless. Police were under-resourced and as frightened as everyone else of those with power. Very often, the police were either helpless or in the pay of those with something to hide.

From the 1970s onwards, the body count began to rise. At first it was priests and peasants. Then it was the lawyers, union leaders and activists. According to Brazil's respected Pastoral Land Commission, hired killers murdered 39 people in 1975 across the Amazon. The numbers rose slowly at first—44 in 1976, 51 in 1977. By the early 1980s, hired killers called *pistoleiros*, *capangas* and *jagunços* were killing hundreds of people every year. There was even a shopping list of prices. It cost a few hundred dollars to arrange for a local activist or union spokesperson to be killed. A judge might cost US$20,000 (A$22,000). When killers hired by wealthy landowners killed Chico Mendes in 1988, he was the fifth rural union president killed during that year. The death of Chico Mendes made headlines because he was known on the international stage. The same is true of Sister Dorothy Stang, an American-Brazilian nun and advocate for the rural poor. Hired assassins gunned her down in 2005. But these well-known deaths were signifiers of a much larger problem. In the state of Pará alone, land conflicts led to 541 murders from 1985 to 2012. Killings everywhere in the Amazon were commonplace. When someone raised this at the 2016 United Nations Climate Conference in Marrakesh, Brazil's agriculture minister Blairo Maggi dismissed the killings. The deaths were, he said, caused by 'problems of personal relationships'.

In Clark's case, most threats were idle. They were a warning, often a form of bravado. Many of them came from those who had drunk too much cachaça, and were forgotten by morning. But how could you tell the difference?

Clark carried on with his project at Xixuaú. The threats didn't stop him. In fact, according to his daughter Cathleen, 'He was never afraid. He might have been sometimes worried about family and situations, about us going through bad situations and him not being able to protect us and stuff like that. But I don't think he has ever been afraid. I've never seen him go back on what he thought was right, or what he was doing because he felt threatened or afraid. Never.'

But whether or not he was afraid, he knew that someone could kill him at any moment. He knew, too, that those doing the killing would, most likely, never be caught. 'We've had a number of murders on this river, and most of them have gone unpunished,' he told me, years after those early threats had passed. 'It's easy for them to disappear. It's easy to hide. It's easy to not be caught.'

～

At one level, things were going well. Tourists were bringing in much-needed money. The school was up and running and other projects were happening. The community was getting stronger and there was a growing sense that everyone at Xixuaú was pulling in the same direction. Everyone was hopeful.

But living in the shadow of constant threats was never easy. And if visits from armed men in uniform became something they learned to live with, shadowy threats from persons unknown were far more frightening. And these were just as much a part of life for Clark and Bonari.

When I spoke with Bonari in 2020, I told her how Clark had made me lie down in the boat on my way back to Novo Airão in 2018, in case Agostinho tried to shoot Clark. She laughed. 'I understand that for you it was a little bit shocking. But we did this a lot with the girls when they were small. We were always going down under the deck, down to the motor where you keep the sacks. When we travelled in the big boat we would go down and wait. Then we would come up to start a normal life again. It was always like that.

'One time when we went to Manaus,' Bonari remembered, 'Chris said, "It's better if you go to Italy." It was a really hard time and we were scared for Chris when he went anywhere, especially to Manaus because it was very easy just to do something to him on the road, and in the middle of people. This happened very often. It was really scary for a long time—for years and years.'

According to Bonari, it was a little easier when they were all at Xixuaú, where Clark always had plenty of friends around him, and local lads were always on the lookout. 'The boys were sleeping at night, but they had eyes even in the backs of their heads, even when they were asleep. Even when we were sleeping, we always knew if there was somebody in the silence or in the dark who arrived. The problem was in Manaus. In the city it was more complicated.'

The worst times of all were when Bonari and their two daughters travelled to Italy, which they did from time to time, and Clark remained behind at Xixuaú. 'It was a really hard time,' Bonari told me, voice breaking. 'We didn't have internet or stuff like that. We could only reach Christopher by phone or with the radio in one of the villages downriver. I used to spend days and nights near to the telephone.'

*You must have wondered if you would ever see him again.*

'Oh yes. Every time the phone rang.'

From 1996 onwards, it was a tense time at Xixuaú, what with all the threats and the tension that arose from Clark's ongoing legal and political problems. Whether or not it was related, Clark's relationship with his brother Paul was also deteriorating further. Disagreements became increasingly heated and turned quickly into full-blown arguments. Paul had always felt that Chris had made a strategic error by not bringing the authorities on board from the beginning, and he saw vindication for this view in the ongoing harassment from Francisco and others. Chris, on the other hand, had less faith in Brazil's political class and saw in Francisco's hostility ironclad proof that he had been wise to go his own way. Paul had also been increasingly unhappy with the way Clark and his companions were running the reserve, and had no time for Clark's friends.

Theirs had always been a complicated relationship. As children, Paul had looked out for his younger brother. Through later life, Paul followed Chris—to Italy, to Brazil, to Xixuaú. Chris was the driving force behind Xixuaú. Perhaps this rankled Paul. Perhaps he felt he had something to prove. Either way, for Paul it was personal in a way that it never was for Chris.

The long-simmering tensions came to a head one dark night in 1998. In Paul's telling, the two brothers drank too much, they both said things they'd later regret, and Paul left soon after with his wife Bianca. Chris told a different story. According to Chris, Paul was voicing his usual criticisms, whereupon Chris told his older brother that if he didn't like the way they were doing things, he was free to leave and do his own thing. Angered, Paul attacked Chris. This was far more than pushing and shoving. Paul grabbed his younger brother by the throat and rained blows down upon him, Chris said. It was a frenzied attack. Chris eventually fought back and landed a few himself. Both men were bloodied and scarred. Chris told his brother to pack his bags and leave. Paul and Bianca were done anyway. They left Xixuaú and never really returned. The two brothers didn't speak to each other for many years afterwards.

Another incident drove a further wedge between Chris and the rest of the Clark family. Clark had found an abandoned farmhouse in Montanero, close to Grosseto in Tuscany, that would become the home for his parents, Colin and Barbara, in their retirement. Paul helped to pour the cement and other building jobs, but it was Chris who oversaw construction of the ten-bedroom home. He was the expert who made the entire project happen. In recognition of all Chris had done, his parents signed an agreement whereby Chris and his family would live rent-free at the house whenever they were in Italy. The agreement also stipulated that Clark would get 20 per cent of the proceeds from any future sale.

When they sold the house for £500,000 (A$1.2 million), Barbara and Colin paid Chris £50,000 (A$125,000), just half of what they had agreed. Clark was livid. It wasn't about the money. He just couldn't believe that his own parents would renege on the deal. Barbara in particular was unyielding. Although she eventually agreed to pay a further £20,000 (A$50,000), she never forgave the slight. Clark and his parents traded accusations and went their separate ways. It was a spectacular falling-out. Most of Clark's siblings sided with their parents. Barbara and Colin moved to Australia. Clark was so angry at what they had done that he didn't speak to his parents for a decade.

Clark's family troubles went even further. He and Bonari had always had a tumultuous relationship. Fireworks were the daily dynamic of their married life, which, over time, became an exhausting round of explosions and recriminations, each one more dramatic than the one before.

Xixuaú was under constant siege, its future uncertain. Clark's life was in danger. And his family life was spiralling out of control, threatening to unravel beyond what could be repaired.

Clark stood at a crossroads in his life.

# 12

# The Golden Years

## *2000–2008*

Xixuaú hung in the balance. It was difficult enough trying to set up a reserve and build a sustainable local community. On top of this, the pressure and threats were becoming intolerable. The popular backlash in Brazil against outside interference that had been building throughout the 1990s had only worsened. In 2001, Mexican–Brazilian writer Lorenzo Carrasco wrote a book called *Máfia Verde* (*Green Mafia*). Clark knew the argument well: 'that the environmental organisations are basically fronts for the rich countries to take over the natural resources of poor countries'. The book found a ready audience, and politicians were only too ready to play to these fears. That Clark was a foreigner made Xixuaú an easy target. Clark was the problem.

In truth, the politicians needed no schooling in the politics of fear. Even before the book appeared, they ranted and they raved. They sent military expeditions to threaten and to seek evidence of wrongdoing. In Francisco's case, he filed the complaints that led to Clark and the association fronting a series of parliamentary inquiries. No accusation became too outrageous. There were, they said, communication antennae in the treetops at Xixuaú. As with the earlier accusations that Clark and his foreigner friends had secret laboratories in the jungle, there were outlandish claims that they had evicted locals from their homes and were presiding over a reign of terror. Clark remembered how rumours from unnamed sources spread that 'we were mistreating and enslaving the local people worse than the most nefarious and bloodthirsty rubber barons of over a century before. We were accused of having clandestine laboratories, of extracting secrets and selling them to Swiss multinational pharmaceutical companies,' Clark told me. 'Because I knew Mikhail Gorbachev and we'd exchanged cards, he and I had an ecological guerrilla camp here in the Xixuaú. They even gave it a name. It was the Green Helmets. Gorbachev and I were training ecological guerrillas. We had massive drug plantations here. Anything you could think of, we were accused of it.'

In September 2000, Clark and his close friend Plinho were summoned to Brasília for a day of hearings before a federal parliamentary inquiry into Xixuaú. They had no choice but to attend. On the morning of the hearings, news came through to them at their hotel that the hearings had been delayed until later in the afternoon. At something of a loose end, Clark and Plinho decided to go for a walk down to the Ministry of the Environment. They had no appointment, and didn't really have a plan. But they were in Brasília and they had time on their hands, so they just turned up. As Clark told me, 'We wandered down the esplanade to the ministry and said, "Hi, we're from the Amazon, from this place called Xixuaú, and we'd like to talk with somebody because we'd really like to make this place a reserve."' No one quite knew what to do with them. Their approach was, after all, a little unorthodox, even for Brasília.

Somehow, they ended up in the offices of Edison Mileski at the Instituto Brasileiro de Meio Ambiente e dos Recursos Naturais Renováveis (Brazilian Institute of the Environment and Renewable Natural Resources, or IBAMA). IBAMA is Brazil's primary environmental body. It implements and polices the federal government's environmental policies. Clark and Plinho stayed and made their case for around an hour and a half. Mileski seemed receptive. They left the meeting with a document signed by an official saying Clark and Plinho were collaborating with IBAMA in protecting the Jauaperi region. The document even mentioned that IBAMA was considering the possibility of establishing an extractive reserve. Then they returned to the hotel to wait for the hearings to begin.

The hearings couldn't have been more hostile. Among the senators on the panel was Gilberto Mestrinho, the former governor of Amazonas who had cheered on the *garimpeiros* when they had invaded Tukano land in the 1980s. Under the glare of television camera lights, six senators asked Clark and Plinho whether they believed in God, how they were making their millions, and whether they had secret laboratories in the jungle. Clark replied that he was doing nothing of the sort. 'I just happen to like living in the Amazon,' he told the senators. Only one of the senators—Marina Silva, from the state of Acre, a future environment minister and presidential candidate—asked anything even vaguely sensible. Years later, she and Clark bumped into each other at an event in Italy. 'I felt so sorry for you that day!' she told him.

Back at the hearings, the interrogation continued for nearly three hours. 'I was accused of being a secret agent for the Queen of England, here to guarantee the resources of this area for the British Crown, like some environmental 007,' Clark recalled. 'Can you imagine the Queen of England wanting the resources of this area?'

*Do you have any dealings with multinational pharmaceutical companies and are you selling them secrets from the Amazon?*

'No, we don't, and no we're not!'

*Do you have an ecological guerrilla training camp with Mikhail Gorbachev?*

'No, we *don't*!'

*How much marijuana do you produce a year?*

'We don't produce *any* marijuana!'

And on it went. The hearings resolved nothing, and the committees never produced a verdict or a report, despite a legal requirement that they do so. Perhaps they never intended to. Perhaps their purpose was just to intimidate. Clark had his own view. 'What they do is just drag it out and leave it open, so if one day they want to come back and get you again, they've got an opening to do that: *Actually, we didn't find in his favour, we didn't find against him. There were still some doubts. Let's go clarify them again now.*'

Clark and Plinho returned to Xixuaú none the wiser as to their fate. But one good thing did come from their trip to the capital. Seven months later, in April 2001, IBAMA's Edison Mileski turned up in Xixuaú on a fact-finding mission. He liked what he saw. He promised to set the wheels in motion at the Ministry for a reserve to be created at Xixuaú. But he wanted a change. Clark and the association had hoped for a reserve that would cover 70,000, perhaps 80,000 hectares (700–800 square kilometres). After travelling and consulting widely throughout the Jauaperi region, Mileski disagreed. No, he said, it should be much bigger. How about half a million hectares?[5]

Although the threats continued, life at Xixuaú improved with each passing year. The visit to Xixuaú by IBAMA in 2001 had given Clark new hope that a reserve might be possible. By 2002, the parliamentary inquiries into Clark and his colleagues were losing momentum. Clark and his friends had even earned a grudging respect among those who pursued them. In a phrase that those involved at Xixuaú loved to repeat years later, one Brazilian politician who opposed them summed up the frustration: 'The more we batter you, the stronger you become.' Despite the best efforts of Brazil's government lawyers, the unusual legal framework used by Clark and Miguel Barrella to create the association held. At a national level, too, things were getting better. Luiz Inácio Lula da Silva of the Workers' Party won the presidential election in 2003. What gave people in the Amazon real hope was that Lula appointed as his environment minister one of their own, Marina Silva. Silva had a record of advocating for the environment and for the people of the Amazon. It felt like a new era.

Clark, Bonari and their two daughters had seen Xixuaú as their real home for a very long time, but they had never made the move permanent. For more than a decade, Clark had been moving back and forth between Europe and Brazil as often as six times a year. Sometimes the family went with him. Sometimes they remained in Italy. For their daughters, Cathleen and Nicolle, it was the most wonderful childhood, but it also cast them adrift between two worlds. 'We never had anything permanent in our life,' Cathleen told me in 2020. 'It is difficult for you to ask me, "Where is [your] home?" or "Where did you feel that your home was?" That's not something that ever came.' Home was both Italy and Brazil, and neither.

'It was all very complicated,' she told me, 'because we wanted to have things that children have in Italy and we couldn't, because all of the money went in tickets and travelling and we couldn't understand that very well at the beginning. Now we're just grateful for it, of course.'

Both girls were adults when I spoke with them, but they remembered well how their experiences were so utterly unlike those of their peers. 'I felt a difficulty expressing things to other people,' Cathleen said, speaking from Italy in 2021. 'I never felt that people here could understand me completely and I never felt that people there could understand me completely. When I was younger and I was telling stories, everyone would listen as if what I was talking about was not real. At the end they would ask questions and I would say, "Yeah, they didn't get it."'

Nicolle had a similar experience. 'It was difficult to get my head around where our home was, where reality was, where we came from. People would never understand us completely when we were talking of one reality or the other. It was frustrating because sometimes you wanted to say things, sometimes you wanted to tell stories, and you could see people not understanding what you were trying to say.'

Neither Clark nor Bonari felt much sympathy for these childhood dilemmas. 'Every time we came back home,' Cathleen remembered, 'we used to say how our friends have this or that. And Dad always used to say, "That's not important. They spend their money on that. We buy tickets."' Cathleen sighed. 'We always used to have tickets.'

No one in the family could agree on when they moved definitively to Brazil. Cathleen had the best explanation. 'We did spend many years spending more time in Italy than in Brazil, for school reasons. And then at a certain point, we started doing it the other way around. We started spending more time in Brazil and less time in Italy.' That happened in 2004.

There were many reasons why they finally decided to make Xixuaú their primary residence. One of the most obvious was that they no longer had a home in Italy after Barbara and Colin sold the house in Grosseto and moved to Australia.

In a strange way, family was central to Clark's motivation. As a child, Clark had felt his family home had been, in his words, a prison, but Chris's siblings were even more dysfunctional as adults. Some succumbed to substance abuse. Conflict simmered beneath the surface and spilled over into violent physical confrontations. Some family members spent years not speaking to each other. Towering over it all was Barbara Clark, who, Clark felt, pulled the financial rug out from underneath her own son. It is difficult not to conclude that Clark ended up in the Amazon in part out of a desire to get as far away as possible from his family.

Then there was his marriage. It was a train wreck. Whenever they were in Italy, his wife and mother couldn't stand being in the same room as each other.

The marriage had many good moments. Clark and Bonari both loved the Amazon. Each adored the other just as much as they couldn't stand each other. And their wild love affair would last for 23 years. During that time, it produced two daughters with whom Clark was besotted.

In my time with Clark in Xixuaú, he laughed often but I saw little of the unbridled joy that everyone said had defined him when he was a young man. Except once. It happened on our way back down from Xixuaú in 2018, having passed the uninhabited danger zone where Agostinho was said to lie in wait. Just north of Novo Airão, we stopped at a tourist boat that was anchored close to shore. Cathleen was out on the deck. The moment he saw her, Clark leaped to his feet. Suddenly childlike, he shouted and waved. He was so excited that he nearly capsized the boat.

Back in 2004, Clark saw the move to Xixuaú as a chance to save his marriage. Clark and Bonari were rarely at their best in Italy. They sometimes were at Xixuaú. Maybe, just maybe, they could make it work and give their children a happy family life in the jungle. Aside from his dreams for Xixuaú, this was his greatest desire. Despite everything that had happened—or was it because of it?—he hoped that by moving to Xixuaú, he could finally crack the family code that had eluded him for so long. For all that Barbara and Paul and Anna had hurt him, he never stopped trying to make it work with them. He was unforgiving of his many enemies when it came to Xixuaú, but no matter what his family did, he forgave them all.

Clark hoped that he could save Xixuaú, and, in return, Xixuaú could help to put his family back together again.

Cathleen and Nicolle Clark had the most remarkable childhood. Partly it was where they lived. It was also because Clark believed in giving his children as much freedom as he could. It was as if he said to himself that his own childhood had been so full of limits and strictures and moralising that he was damned if he was going to do the same to his own kids.

'I remember Xixuaú as the best memories ever because our childhood was very free,' Cathleen told me. 'It was always hot, so we could spend as long as we wanted in the water. We could swim, we could paddle around, we were free, we could fish. We could do everything we wanted. And we had so many loving and caring people around us.'

Nicolle felt the same way. 'My father was the funnest father in the world. We had so much fun in our lives. I can imagine if you ask my mum, she will tell you it has been the most embarrassing time of our lives, because Dad had no shame. He would let us do whatever we wanted. He never gave us limits. It was just total freedom. *Just go and have fun.*' Nicolle laughed at the memory. 'He was that kind of person.'

If there was any structure at Xixuaú in those years, it revolved around school. The girls were aged fourteen and eleven at the time of the move in 2004, and Clark made arrangements for them to do distance learning. They connected from time to time via the internet. But for the most part it was home-schooling. Clark taught and tutored his daughters in science, maths and geography. Bonari was responsible for history, art and literature. They learned in both English and Italian, and they were already fluent in Portuguese. Once a year they travelled to Italy for the end-of-year exams.

For the rest of the time, Nicolle and Cathleen were too busy having fun. At Xixuaú, life itself was an education. Their surroundings were endlessly fascinating.

'We were just happy children all the time,' Cathleen said. 'We had this very strange and weird life where we would sometimes fiddle around with an anaconda, or sometimes have snakes around the house and it was just so natural and normal.'

Nicolle went further:

Xixuaú was a magical place, full of tourists from all over the world. It was full of kids. We were a lot of kids. We were always having a lot of fun. There was one huge *maloca*. It was beautiful. All of the people of the village used to come and we would do parties. We would stay all together. It was just amazing. It was like a huge community, a really beautiful community . . . I don't think many people in life can say they've grown up in a place like that. We didn't have light.

We didn't have TV. We didn't have anything like that. We had it when we were in Italy, for example, so we knew things. But we didn't miss them, because back then it was so easy, you know? My mum was there. My dad was there. You didn't really miss anything else. I do remember it as an amazing childhood.

Bonari was fully invested in the lifestyle, but even she couldn't believe her eyes sometimes. 'We used to spend a lot of time in the water playing with Dad,' Nicolle recalled. 'Mum used to go insane, that we would get eaten by a crocodile sooner or later. Mum used freak out and say, "Kids, be careful when you enter the water because, you know, there are many things in the Amazon. Just be careful." And Dad used to say, "Hmph! You are so Italian." And then he'd run and jump in the water, and call out, "Kids, come on!" Oh my god! We'd be like, "Anything could be under there and will eat Dad!"'

Was this a source of tension between Clark and Bonari?

'No, no,' Nicolle confirmed. 'She would actually end up laughing and saying, "Chris, you're mad!"'

For all the faultlines in their marriage, Clark and Bonari were a team. 'He was so extreme in some things and she would balance him,' Nicolle told me. 'She would have all the things that he missed and that he needed. They completed each other. He would give her the adventure part of life and she would give him the stable part of life.'

It was little wonder that the girls' friends back in Italy could scarcely understand the stories they brought back. Among their Italian peers, they were known as 'the mad family'. Such a response was not without reason, and much of it had to do with the local wildlife and the animal stories that emerged from their lives in Brazil.

Clark loved all of the Amazon's creatures. The only possible exception was mosquitoes, but there were few of those at Xixuaú. He defended all creatures' right to be where they wanted. This was their home. It was human beings who didn't belong. Nature must be left to run its course. Even when he was stabbed by a stingray, he blamed himself. Bats were a particular favourite. He steadfastly refused to evict colonies of bats whenever they invaded the family home. He thought they were cute.

What the rest of the family thought of this didn't seem to matter. He loved spiders. When I visited in 2018 and found a giant tarantula in my bathroom, he left it there. It wasn't to frighten me. He just couldn't understand that I might be uncomfortable with the whole idea. Then there were the snakes. Nicolle remembered how once, when she was still small, a snake took up residence right above her pillow. 'I remember asking my dad—"Please, Dad, can you please, *please* take him away from there? I can't sleep with a snake above my head." And he said, "No, come on, it's his house too." So I got my pillow, got my teddy bear, and went to sleep with Mum and Dad. My bed was invaded,' she laughed, 'and he wouldn't move a finger!'

Family friend Tom Haycraft remembered how the Clarks' Amazon life 'was like something out of "Five Go Mad in the Amazon". There was a famous caiman called Lucifer, or Lucy for short. It was outside the big *maloca* on the other side of the river. There was a balsa [platform] there and Lucy would come every evening to the balsa, and she'd come right up to the platform. And the girls would just be sitting there, gutting fish, and we'd chuck mouthfuls to this enormous bloody crocodile. And then we'd all swim in the river. Nobody was afraid of anything.'

It would never have occurred to Clark to be afraid.

'Dad was just born for the forest,' Cathleen told me. 'He was a forest man since the beginning. He'd have nothing to do with Occidental life, with European life. Sometimes we would think: *What happened to this man?*'

For all their strangeness, these were golden years for the family. Clark was at ease here. His friends would later remember that Clark was happiest at Xixuaú, and they never saw him happier than during those years.

'I remember spending long hours in hammocks talking and drinking caipirinhas with Chris,' Haycraft recalled. 'That was the peak time—everybody was united, everybody was following the same course. There was no division within the community. Occasionally people would get pissed off, but it was very much a community.'

Things were moving forward in other ways, too. In addition to eradicating malaria, Clark and the others had set up a program to eliminate intestinal parasites and worms from Xixuaú and the surrounding areas. People were living longer. The community had money like never before, thanks to a steady flow of visiting tourists. The installation of a satellite dish and an internet connection made other things possible. In 2006, Clark arranged for the community to have its first television set, powered by a generator, so that everyone could watch the football World Cup. Clark was reluctant. He knew that a television was a corrupting influence, that it would cause locals to spend more time watching *telenovelas* from Rio and São Paulo than they would spend in the jungle. But he also knew that it would happen one day, whether he brought it or not. During the World Cup, at least, the TV sat in the middle of the village and everyone at Xixuaú crowded around the set and enjoyed the games together. 'It was almost more interesting watching them watching television, than watching the television itself,' Clark remembered.

There were more serious benefits, especially when it came to having a reliable internet connection. Clark lost count of the number of machete wounds that he sewed back together after seeking medical advice from doctors on a satellite connection with Europe. On one occasion, two local teenage boys went out fishing. When a duck flew over, one grabbed a rifle to shoot it. The trigger caught on something and the gun went off, shooting the boy in the head. By the time the two young men arrived back in the village, the one with the head injury was in a bad way. Using the internet connection, Clark called a friend in Italy, who in turn patched through a call to a surgeon in Pisa. Over the next two hours, Clark ran between the injured boy at the health post and the surgeon on the line. Following the surgeon's instructions, Clark was able to stabilise the terrified youth and treat the wounds. Once stabilised, the young man was taken downriver to hospital and survived.

On board a small riverboat at sunrise on Lake Maicá, close to Santarém.
ANTHONY HAM

Giant lily pads on an arm of Lake Maicá, a few hundred metres from the main branch of the Amazon. ANTHONY HAM

Even close to a city like Santarém, undisturbed forest on the margins of Lake Maicá can feel like wilderness. ANTHONY HAM

The boundaries between water and dry land are often blurred in the Amazon, as they are here on Lake Maicá. ANTHONY HAM

In a time of flood, water levels rise across the Amazon, creating islands where once there were grassy plains. ANTHONY HAM

The birds of Lake Maicá: (*top*) chestnut-fronted macaws in flight, and (*bottom*) egrets flying across the lake. Waterbirds in particular benefit from high water levels during the flood season. ANTHONY HAM

Floodwaters inundate seasonal fishing villages and encampments on Lake Maicá; structures such as this need to be rebuilt every year. ANTHONY HAM

Lake Maicá: (*top*) Sunrise is a time of quiet beauty, still waters and soft light; (*middle*) the forest presses close to the shoreline; (*bottom*) one of many islands created by rising floodwaters, July 2018. ANTHONY HAM

The interplay of water and forest stretching to the horizon is a common sight in the Amazon, as here on Lake Maicá (*top*); a black-collared hawk keeps a lookout for prey on the lake (*bottom*). ANTHONY HAM

Even though this appears to be the water's edge, waters extend far beyond the wall of trees when the river is in flood.  ANTHONY HAM

Colourful forest birds like the turquoise tanager are a feature of life in the Amazon.
ANTHONY HAM

Most mammals in the Amazon have adapted to live part of their lives in the trees, especially during the flood season. ANTHONY HAM

Iguanas are cold blooded and like to sun themselves in the trees, especially along river edges in the morning. ANTHONY HAM

A forest path through the Floresta Nacional do Tapajós, south of Santarém.
ANTHONY HAM

Looking down on the forest canopy from an observation tower in the Floresta Nacional do Tapajós. ANTHONY HAM

The meeting of the waters at Santarém, where the Tapajós, a clearwater river, meets the muddy, brown waters of the main Amazon. ANTHONY HAM

A red howler monkey, one of the most charismatic and vocal primates of the Amazon. ANTHONY HAM

In the Amazon, it always pays to look up: (*left*) a southern tamandua; (*below*) a hoatzin, one of the most unusual birds in the Amazon, described by one naturalist as having 'a spiky crest like a punk haircut'. It calls in a variety of ways, including low grunts.
ANTHONY HAM

A black caiman suns itself on the banks of a tributary of the main Amazon River.
ANTHONY HAM

Brown-throated sloths have limited mobility, but the interaction of algae and lichens with a sloth's fur ensures they're well camouflaged. ANTHONY HAM

Chris Clark fills the tank at a floating petrol station in Novo Airão, in readiness for our trip to Xixuaú. ANTHONY HAM

Chris Clark's wooden home surrounded by floodwaters on the banks of the lagoon at Xixuaú. ANTHONY HAM

The guest quarters, where I slept for nearly two weeks, just across the water from Clark's home at Xixuaú. ANTHONY HAM

Valdemar walking through the village of Xixuaú.
ANTHONY HAM

Shenaya, daughter of Chris Clark and Artemizia, with one of her cousins at Xixuaú. ANTHONY HAM

The children of Xixuaú.
ANTHONY HAM

Valdemar cleans a pirarucú, one of the Amazon's largest fish, on the back deck of Clark's home in Xixuaú. ANTHONY HAM

Chris Clark on the deck of his home. ANTHONY HAM

Clark and his family cross the lagoon to Xixuaú village to deliver Agostinho's police summons to the village vice-president. ANTHONY HAM

A traditional family home made from local materials in the village of Xixuaú.
ANTHONY HAM

Valdemar paddles a canoe through the waters around Xixuaú. ANTHONY HAM

A storm approaches near the entrance to the lagoon. ANTHONY HAM

The great cloud banks that form over the Amazon rainforest, reflected in the waters of the Rio Jauaperi, close to Xixuaú. ANTHONY HAM

It can be difficult to differentiate between sky and water when the Jauaperi is still and calm. ANTHONY HAM

In the flooded Amazon forest, there is no dry land for months at a time.
ANTHONY HAM

The late-afternoon light on the Rio Jauaperi, close to Xixuaú. ANTHONY HAM

Clark eventually reconciled with his older brother, and Paul Clark and Valdemar soon had a major success. Chris had always had his eye on the bigger prize of getting the reserve declared. When Paul and Valdemar visited the IBAMA offices in Manaus in 2006, the local delegate told them that any reserve could still be years away. Through their persistence, Paul and Valdemar were able to get the east bank of the Jauaperi included in the reserve proposal. More immediately, they pushed through an agreement that closed the river to commercial fishing until a study of fish stocks could happen. The initial agreement was for three years, but no such study was ever carried out, and the agreement effectively remains in place until this day.

Deforestation had also slowed under the administration of President Lula, and in 2006 the Amazon Soy Moratorium (ASM) came into force. It was by no means a perfect document, and implementation would always be problematic. But international conservation groups hailed it as the Amazon's first major zero-deforestation agreement. Under its terms, soybean producers would be unable to sell their harvest if it came from land that had been deforested after 2006. Two years later, Lula's government set up the Fund for the Amazon using US$100 million (A$145 million) from Norway. The Fund was designed to support scientific studies and contribute to sustainable development projects.

Not everything worked.

Every attempt in Xixuaú to set up a farm to make the community self-sufficient failed. A permaculture experiment met the same fate. The combination of infertile soils, an unforgiving climate, and a formidable population of fungi and parasites forced them to abandon any crop-growing. Clark was undaunted: 'As far as failures go, it was a most interesting failure.'

At a national level, for all the progress made and the best efforts of Marina Silva, Lula's attention rarely attached to the Amazon and its people, and the Amazon remained under existential threat. According to authors Maurício Torres and Sue Branford, Lula's 'social policies, widely praised for tackling the country's historic problem of profound inequality, were directed mainly to the poor living on the margins of large cities. The difficulties faced by indigenous and traditional communities were never a priority for Lula.' Partly because of this, Marina Silva resigned as environment minister in 2008.

Other Lula policies had unintended consequences. One initiative paid people not to fish in parts of the Amazon during the season when fish were breeding. All of a sudden, everyone was a fisherman. Where before just a handful of people fished on the Jauaperi, and always for subsistence, hundreds now took advantage of the scheme. Worst of all, because the money was paid during the breeding season, it became the only time of year when people had enough money to pay for the diesel to get a boat up the river, and the only time they had money for the ice and the ice boxes to store all the fish. Lula's well-intentioned scheme ended up having the opposite effect.

Issues began to arise in the Clarks' family life as well. She may have enjoyed a wonderful childhood, but Nicolle was now a teenager and the novelty was wearing thin. 'When I was fifteen, I wanted to run away from that place. It was so small. Everyone knew everything about everyone else. There was no privacy, no private room. There was, like, ten in one house, and I was like, "Dad, Mum, we *have* to leave this place.'"

Clark and Bonari, too, found it increasingly difficult to paper over the cracks in their marriage. The problems that had driven them apart in Italy and elsewhere eventually followed them to Xixuaú. 'It was always very dramatic,' Cathleen told me years later. 'Everything was full of emotions all the time.' No one knew when those emotions would spill over into something more serious.

It remains true nonetheless that the period from 2002 to 2008 was the golden age for Clark and his family. Indeed, they were their own version of the Tolstoyan mantra: whether happy or unhappy, they were utterly unlike any other family.

And besides, when it came to Xixuaú, they seemed to be on the cusp of something remarkable, as Clark well knew. 'Those were the years of real development and progress in the Xixuaú,' he told me. 'The political attacks had died down and we had requested the creation of the extractive reserve. The environment ministry was working on it. We were protecting the environment, and the standard of living of the people of Xixuaú was rising as tourism and other projects brought income, education, health and social projects.'

Things were heading in the right direction, and they seemed on the verge of meaningful and lasting change.

# 13

# Things Fall Apart

*2008–2010*

There are always many sides to a story. Only those who are present during events can really know what occurred. Even then, each will have their own version. But I have spoken with most of those involved. And I have read Clark's journal from the period.

In our conversations, Clark was always very discreet. To outsiders like me, he often brushed over less salubrious details. Or he steered the conversation away from anything that would give a less flattering image of a friend or family member. But Clark felt profoundly hurt by his perception of the conduct of his mother, his brother Paul, and Anna Bonari towards him. Each time, he spiralled into drink and despair.

Once, he wrote, 'I stepped off the cliff edge again and found myself hurtling through space in total freefall looking desperately around for something to grab hold of.' On one occasion, he found himself 'reeling around, bloodied and dazed, knowing neither how to stop nor how to continue'. Yet another time in Xixuaú, Clark was so blinded with rage and hurt at a betrayal that he took up an axe and tried to destroy the lodge that he and his colleagues had spent years building. Only a well-aimed punch in the jaw from Erik, his closest friend, stopped his fury. I suspect, too, that for much of his life Clark was a borderline alcoholic. But then each time he picked himself up and carried on. It was the most British thing about him.

I learned very few of these things from Clark himself, at least not directly. It took time for me to join the dots between the Clark I knew—calm, diplomatic, in control—and the angry, sometimes desperately unhappy man who wrote down his innermost thoughts in his journal. In person, Clark came across as measured and thoughtful. One on one, he saved his anger for the Trumps of this world, or those who were the enemies of Xixuaú.

His journals painted an entirely different picture. There he was foul-mouthed and furious, open about his bouts of despair and, it must be said, often disbelieving about perceived betrayals from those who should have been on his side. Doubtless we are all like this. Surely we all present a different face to the world at times. The challenge for me here is to accurately convey what happened. To read Clark's journals was a privilege, granted to me by a family keen that the legacy of Clark's life be told. What I learned from reading the journals helped me understand Clark better. It showed him to be deeply flawed, yes. But it made him more human.

In 2008, Clark and Anna Bonari finally separated.

When I asked Clark about what happened, he batted away the question. 'My wife actually became quite involved for a time,' he told me. 'But it was never really what she wanted and she couldn't quite find the right role for herself.' He spoke about how they grew apart, as if they had drifted organically along separate paths until they could no longer find their way back together. The version he told me doesn't square with what I later learned. Perhaps if I had known him longer, he might have told me more. In his journal, he was more forthcoming. His marriage was, he wrote, 'more riddled with holes than Emmental cheese'.

When I asked Bonari for her version, she told me that she loved Xixuaú, that she considered it to be home, and that she never found true happiness after she returned to Europe. Nicolle put it another way: 'She loved that place and she loved everything. She just didn't feel appreciated enough.'

Bonari told me that it was all about their daughters. In her telling, she reached a point where she wanted Cathleen and Nicolle to have a proper education. Clark, she said, only had eyes for Xixuaú and he couldn't see that his daughters were growing up and needed more than a jungle education. 'I'd say, "Chris, you have to think about this. We have two children. They have a future and we have to think about what they are going to do. We have to spend time in Italy so when they grow up, they can decide." But that was too much and Chris didn't have time to do that. He was focused on his business at Xixuaú. He also didn't have much time to think about me or Cathleen or Niky in many ways. I've always been thinking about Cathleen and Niky, because he's always been too busy with Xixuaú.'

Clark knew his limitations better than perhaps anyone realised. And Bonari wasn't entirely wrong about Clark having eyes only for the bigger picture. In his journal, Clark wrote:

I have never had time for the small problems of people and I realize that this is a major character flaw of mine. Every human being has small problems and needs someone to listen to them about them. I am not that person and Anna has always punished me for that. The people here have long learned not to come to me with their little problems. The wife or husband has been unfaithful, someone said something offensive, someone broke something small of theirs. I am not the person they come to. Sick children, food supplies, money to buy the things they need, these are the things I deal with.

Even so, Bonari was, I think, wrong to suggest that she was the one who was most concerned with trying to build a life that was best for their daughters. Others remember it differently. Clark and Bonari engaged in some truly spectacular and explosive arguments, but they held it together for the kids whenever they could. One family member remembered that it was Clark, more than Bonari, who tried the hardest to protect their daughters from the hurt caused by a disintegrating marriage. 'He was all about his daughters. He lived for that and everything was for that.' Nicolle told me also that 'his life was based on us. He did everything from the perspective of thinking, *I want a better future for them. I want this place to be a place where they can live.*'

Most likely there is some truth in Bonari's accusation that Clark was blind to the family's need for a world beyond Xixuaú. But that was because he thought that they had everything they needed at Xixuaú, and that the rest would take care of itself. This difference in approach and perspective almost certainly played a role in their drifting apart. But that's not why they separated. The move to Xixuaú had only detoured temporarily around the chasms that already lay between Clark and Bonari. It only postponed the inevitable. There were many causes to their final separation: the fights, the lies, the accusations. Who knows where the tipping point lay? Whatever it was, what had once been tumultuous was now toxic. Many years later, Nicolle told me: 'Dad was one of those men who would never split up from Mum. Never in life. He loved her too much. He would have accepted everything.'

In the end, the separation played out in a way that was as complicated as the family's life had always been. Clark took off for Italy with Nicolle. 'I went to Italy with him when they split up,' Nicolle remembered. 'But he never told me that they were divorcing. He just told me that Mum was busy with her projects there, and Cathleen stayed there and we were going to Italy because I had to go to school. And these were, I think, three of the happiest months of my life. We had so much fun, me and Dad, in Italy. So he never had the courage to tell me what was happening. When Mum arrived—because they met in São Paulo, he went back with Cathleen and she came to Italy—in one week she told me everything. So, suddenly, my whole world collapsed.'

The family went their separate ways. The happy family life

that Clark had craved had been a chimera. They had always divided their lives between Italy and Brazil. Now their family was forever split along the same lines.

Whatever the cause, when the marriage fell apart, so too did Clark. Something died within him when Bonari left him. It wasn't just that he grieved. It went further than that.

'Mum broke him when she left Xixuaú,' Nicolle told me. 'The break-up broke his heart. He loved Mum so much, and he loved the concept of family. He lived for us. That was the breaking moment for him. After that there have been bits and pieces of my dad doing things, but it never worked again as efficiently as it was before, when he was whole.'

'He was quieter,' Cathleen remembered of those dark times. 'He was less happy, of course. He just started living day by day and not working much on his projects. He used to cry more, in the early morning.'

When I knew Clark, he was wise and witty and somewhat resigned to the vagaries of human nature. I didn't understand until later how different he had been when he had first arrived in Brazil. As a younger man, he had been a free spirit and a visionary. There is a photo of Clark as this younger man. In the photo he is not so much walking as appearing to leap on water, his arms outstretched, long hair flowing. It is an image that captures the pure, unadulterated joy that Clark's younger self felt and projected whenever he was in the Amazon. The photo, Cathleen told me, 'expressed exactly what he thought and how he felt in Brazil—free and happy'.

In some ways, his greatest achievements would come in the years after he and Bonari separated. But according to those who knew him the longest, the joy of life left him when his family fell apart for the final time.

With Bonari and Nicolle gone from Xixuaú, Clark began drinking. It would start not long after he got up in the morning and continue until late at night. There was always a cigarette in his hand. He stopped taking care of himself. Only Cathleen, who was then eighteen, could touch him. Just when it seemed that he was digging a hole from which he might not be able to emerge, Cathleen would pull him back out. As Nicolle told it, 'Cathleen was always there, always there. When it was just too much, she was just, "Okay, enough. This is too much, Dad."' No one else could reach him. But he listened to Cathleen.

'We all have characters that do tend towards addictions,' Nicolle told me. 'That's just reality. Only Cathleen doesn't. It's horrible. At least Dad always said, "I know I have this tendency. I know I have to step backward. I know that I cannot let myself go because I have more important things to do."'

It wasn't just the end of his marriage that nearly destroyed Clark.

Since 1996, when local politician Francisco had arrived on the scene, Clark's life had been in constant danger. For more than a decade, these threats had come from outside the Xixuaú and Jauaperi communities—they had come from state or federal politicians and their hired thugs. Clark had stared down the threats to his life and withstood the interminable parliamentary commissions of inquiry. Over time, these threats had receded: Roraima's politicians remained unhappy with Clark and with the very idea of giving over more state land to conservation, but their opposition had petered out. For the most part, when he was at Xixuaú, Clark felt safe.

It was around the time the final act of Clark's marriage was playing out that President Lula struck a deal with the state of Roraima. If Roraima gave up their fight over Xixuaú (along with a handful of other tracts of land), then the federal government would hand over six million hectares—60,000 square kilometres—of federal land to state control. Roraima grumbled, but they knew a good deal when they saw it. At the stroke of a pen, all threats to Clark from the state politicians ended.

Looking back in 2018, Clark understood that the threats had been less about him than political expedience. 'You can't expect to be responsible for the creation of a massive protected area in a foreign country like this without having somebody hating your guts for it. Lots of politicians from Roraima hated me. Lots of local politicians,' he told me. 'But a politician's hate in Brazil is not a personal hate. The politicians will hate you. They might even kill you. But it's only if they think it's in their own interests. It was not in their interests anymore, so the politicians lost interest in persecuting us. They got their deal. As far as they're concerned, they can go to their people and say, "We got a really good deal—over six million hectares for giving up one million hectares [10,000 square kilometres]. We've done a good job." There was absolutely no reason for them to persecute or hate me anymore. Even the very first one who started it—Francisco—he's still our local representative and we're friends today.'

Roraima's acceptance of Lula's offer should have been cause for celebration, and everyone at Xixuaú certainly toasted developments with a cachaça or caipirinha or two. But as the threat from external forces receded, threats from within the community were growing.

In 2010 or 2011 when Clark was in Italy, he went to the bank on Xixuaú business. There he discovered that someone had changed all of the passwords to the accounts. He also heard from Xixuaú that, in his absence, someone had turned the local community against him by claiming that he was stealing money from the association. It could never be proven who was behind it all. Whoever had done it, the effect was that Clark had been ousted from any position of leadership or responsibility in the community. It was nothing short of a coup d'état. That it was able to succeed owed everything to the nature of the community at Xixuaú. Clark and the whole idea of a reserve had put down deep roots among those who lived at Xixuaú. But as with marginal communities everywhere, the ongoing support of locals depended on their own financial situation. Clark was on the cusp of something extraordinary and had carried the community along with him. But it was still fragile, and subject to outside manipulation. No one had become rich in Xixuaú and most people there still lived precariously close to poverty. Others had also come in, drawn to the opportunities, but they had no ties to, or awareness of, Clark's vision for the reserve.

'I think they were at the point where people were starting to understand that it was better to learn how to build an environment that would have been sustainable in time because it was giving them money,' Nicolle told me. 'It was full of tourists. It was full of activities that were giving them money. But when your condition goes backward just a little bit, and you feel you're hungry again for even one day, you will start living exactly like you were living ten years ago, because it was the easy way of living.'

When Clark returned to Xixuaú from Italy, his marriage lay in ruins and his involvement in Xixuaú hung in the balance. No wonder he fell, and fell hard.

'They just broke him,' Nicolle said. 'The whole breaking up of Dad started there. He came to Italy because he was divorcing from my mum. When he came back, they had cut him out of *every*thing. Everything that was his lifetime job.'

'He actually had to reinvent his whole life,' Cathleen agreed. 'Suddenly after they split, he lost a lot of his strength. He lost the association not long after that as well, so he went down, down, down, down, down.'

Every tragic hero has his or her dark night of the soul. This was Clark's. In the course of a few years, the two great loves of his life—his family and Xixuaú—had been taken from him. He abandoned the *maloca* that had been at the heart of his vision for Xixuaú for years. He moved across the lagoon. There he built a small hut and licked his wounds. Then he descended into a pit of despair from which his family feared he would never emerge.

# 14

# Requiem for Nature

*2010–2016*

The community at Xixuaú had turned against Clark. His personal life was a mess. And nearly two decades after he first imagined the reserve, the project at Xixuaú seemed to be going nowhere.

Clark had achieved more than most people do in a lifetime. He and his colleagues had partnered with the Waimiri-Atroari to extend the area where the Amazon's trees and other wildlife enjoyed a measure of protection. They had effectively eradicated malaria, and had brought the internet, schools and health posts to remote communities without altering their essential fabric.

But by 2010, Clark was fragile and in danger of descending into dark places from which he may have never returned. For a while, Xixuaú would have to wait.

A difficult life can go either way. It breaks some people.

It fortifies others. Despite everything—despite a constricting childhood, a broken and occasionally violent relationship with his brother, his mother's betrayal, countless threats to his life and a failed marriage—Clark had never passed the point of no return. Whatever it was that he clung to throughout these trials down through the years served him well now as his life's dream at Xixuaú began to slip from his grasp. Cathleen's presence, too, helped to keep him from disappearing entirely into alcohol-fuelled disintegration, and through the fog of grief and betrayal and intoxication, Clark somehow kept despair at bay. He knew that he had come too far to give up now. He couldn't dwell on the past. And so it was that Clark picked himself up and forged ahead with his projects, battling his demons as he went.

To fund what he wanted to do, he built up his own tourism company called Visit Amazonia. Still broken by what had happened, he managed to find purpose again in his life. 'He built Visit Amazonia in two years,' Nicolle Clark remembered. 'He rebuilt it himself completely. It wasn't the association he dreamt of. But he knew it was something that was having success. It was something people were loving. He was really happy about it. No one else could have rebuilt his entire life like that in two years. It was such a creative thing, and so deeply connected to what he wanted to do.'

Clark's vision for Xixuaú had always been equal parts community-building and environmental protection. Building a community in such a place was always going to be Clark's greatest challenge, and it's one that he never quite mastered. In some ways, it would always remain the great unfinished project of his life.

Clark always tried to involve the local community as much as he could. But under the new regime, and with money coming in from other sources, Clark found many in the community to be unreliable. 'People wanted money for nothing. They didn't understand that this project could only happen if people worked hard. I'm not going to work with somebody who goes out with a tourist at 7.30 a.m. and is back by 8.15 a.m. You can't work for me like that.'

Now that he was less involved in community life, Clark had time to think. As he always had, he wrestled with the bigger issues that arose on the frontline where tradition, community development and survival in the modern world came together. A school had always been a pillar of his vision for the community. He only had to look at Valdemar, who had been so desperate for his children to learn to read and write. The school had been Clark's idea, and although the building of that school was a communal project to which many people contributed, it remains part of Clark's legacy. This is to take nothing away from his brother, Paul. If Chris Clark was the driving force behind the whole school idea, Paul kept it going. In the words of Tom Haycraft, Paul 'educated a whole generation of *caboclo* kids'. Whatever their disagreements, Chris Clark was quick to recognise his older brother's contribution as teacher. 'Paul has the merit of having built the only school on the river that has ever worked,' Nicolle Clark told me. 'He has been a remarkable teacher in Jauaperi. That's not something that Dad ever questioned.'

And yet, as formal education grew at Xixuaú, something was, inevitably, being lost in the education of the local children. As soon as he could walk, Valdemar had followed his father around, absorbing essential bush knowledge. He was a *mateiro*, which translates loosely as a 'person of the forest'. That's how children learned back then. Very often, it was all that they needed. Not anymore. Whether the young people of Xixuaú and Jauaperi stayed in the forest or moved to Manaus and beyond, a basic school education was now a minimum requirement.

At the same time, the hours that the children spent in school in Xixuaú and in Gaspar was time that they no longer spent in the forest. Life beyond the schoolroom had changed, too. 'Now nearly everyone's got a television set in their home,' Clark told me. 'And there's a generator that serves the whole village. The kids get up in the morning, go to school at 7.15 a.m., get out at 11, come home, have lunch, the generator goes on, and they sit themselves down in front of the television. There are no longer children becoming jungle men or jungle women. The whole way of living has completely and utterly changed. Most of the 30-year-olds here, from the age of three onwards, would get up in the morning and whatever their father was doing, they were with their father. So they learned jungle knowledge—they learned to hunt, they learned to fish. Most of the fathers aren't jungle people any more. They sit idle on government assistance.

'But what do you do?' he said after a pause. 'Not put the schools in?'

Of course not.

'Where are the future jungle men?' he continued. 'Where are the future *mateiros* going to come from? Nobody has an answer to that question. And if these guys are not *mateiros* in the jungle, what are they? Impoverished, marginal individuals. There's no future for them. They'll never get on in life unless their knowledge is valued. To all the scientists who come here, and all the researchers who come here, these guys are just labour, somebody to row them around and take them to see the animal they want to see. Television companies could never film the animals if it wasn't for the people who know where the animals are, know how to get them close enough to the animals to film them. But nobody gives it any value. And they're losing their knowledge. Their skills are being lost from generation to generation.'

Clark never ceased to ask these questions. But now that he had suffered a form of exile from the community he had helped to create, the answers eluded him more than ever.

In around 2010, Clark married Artemizia, one of Valdemar's daughters. It further complicated Clark's life amid the feuds that were never far away. Valdemar and Paul Clark later became sworn enemies, and Clark would find himself in the impossible position of having to choose between his brother and his father-in-law. But that lay in the future. Two years after they married, Artemizia gave birth to a baby girl, whom they called Shenaya.

Shenaya was six when I arrived in Xixuaú in 2018, and she was a gorgeous, precocious little girl who brought much happiness to everyone who knew her. Clark's heart would melt every time she batted her eyelids at him, and he gave in often over Artemizia's protests. Shenaya would leap into the water out the front of the hut, squealing in delight while Clark watched on with an adoring smile.

Although I never saw them together, Cathleen and Nicolle similarly adored their younger sister, and they felt deeply protective towards her. Because of this, they were intensely critical of their father, and of how he had let himself go. They remembered what Clark had been like when they were young. The father of a young daughter they now saw was a shadow of the father he once had been. 'He just decided to live as a native in the middle of the forest, day by day,' Cathleen said. 'He didn't teach any other language to his younger daughter, to my sister, just Portuguese, and she grew up completely as a local. She knows no other life, other than a local Indian life. We criticised him a lot for that. He just had no strength left to fight anymore. He fought in his own way. But not like he used to do.'

Nicolle told me a similar story, confirming that Clark was no longer the man he once had been, and he probably knew it. 'I can identify the moments of our life that have changed him,' said Nicolle. She spoke of Clark's separation from her mother. She identified the coup that removed him from the day-to-day running of Xixuaú. The birth of Shenaya, Nicolle said, belonged in the same category, albeit for very different reasons. 'When Shenaya arrived, he was completely aware of the fact that he was not capable of raising a kid like he was with us. He was so full of energy when we were kids. We travelled a lot. We could go camping every weekend. He would find amazing places for us to go. He was just not energetic enough when she arrived. And he knew it. He knew that he couldn't give her what she deserved. And that's true—she doesn't speak English, she doesn't speak Italian, she has a pretty common, standard Brazilian education. And that's not what he would want for one of his daughters. He never wanted that.'

With everything that was happening, a strong and healthy community may now have been beyond Clark's reach. But he could still protect the environment.

In doing so, Clark still knew how to have an adventure. And he still had plenty of crazy ideas. He worried that nothing was happening, that vital momentum had been lost. By 2014, he was getting desperate, scouting around for something dramatic that would call attention to the plight of the Amazon, and the need to protect Xixuaú and places like it. Although deforestation had fallen across the Brazilian Amazon by 18 per cent in 2013–14, this came after years of record increases. The slowing of forest clearance was a blip, and the rate of deforestation began again to accelerate. At around this time, an Italian film director named Giancarlo Cammerini was visiting. Cammerini fell in love with the place and Clark told him his idea.

'When the beaches are out, in low water, in the middle of the river here, it's incredibly beautiful—you can't imagine.

You've got the jungle on either side, you're on a beach in the middle, and, at the right water level if you take photos, it looks like you're walking on water. I would love to have a Pink Floyd concert, there, at that time.'

Clark thought no more about it—or, if he did, he'd enjoy the idea for a while then dismiss it as something that he knew could never happen.

Cammerini wasn't so sure. He wrote up the idea, entered it in a joint Brazilian–Italian film-funding competition, and won. In 2018, Clark recounted what happened next. 'They got in touch with David Gilmour, and David Gilmour said that he was interested in the Amazon, but he would never play with Roger Waters again. Then, about six months ago, Roger Waters said he wanted to do a Wall concert, between America and Mexico because of Trump's plan to build a wall, and that he was open to a reunion of Pink Floyd. So now they want me to go to London and talk with Roger Waters and present this idea to him. For me, it would be like a *Requiem for Nature*, a *Requiem for the Natural World*. Who better than for Pink Floyd to do something like that?'

The film never happened. And Pink Floyd never did get back together again. But before the project died, in December 2015 Cammerini turned up in the Amazon with a film crew to scout locations and generally push the project along. On 5 December, Clark, Cammerini and the film crew travelled downriver from Xixuaú, then on to São Paulo, Rio de Janeiro and Brasília for meetings with government officials. Although they didn't know it at the time, two days after they left, on 7 December, four young men from Xixuaú crossed the

Jauaperi in a canoe to go fishing. They lit a fire, cooked their catch, then returned to Xixuaú. It was one of the driest dry seasons in living memory, and because they didn't put the fire out properly, it took hold. Three days later, one of the four saw the fire on the horizon, and raised the alarm in the village, but no one would go with him to help put it out. He battled alone for a whole day, but the fire front was already 100 metres across. Looking back three years after the event, Clark remembered how, when similar fires had happened before, 'I have got every man in the village, and we have sometimes spent two full days putting the fire out. We'd come back a week later and realise it wasn't out, and so we'd go back and spend another two full days doing this. Nobody did a damn thing. Nobody said anything to anybody.'

Every year, fires create catastrophic levels of destruction across the Amazon. Clark scoffed at the idea that most fires began naturally, as the government sometimes claimed. 'Most of the fires in the Amazon are *not* natural. They're almost always started by some idiot. They're clearing to plant and don't put the fire out. That's how they normally start in the Amazon. They're all human-made. Not necessarily deliberately. People just don't care. When it's dry is when you clear and burn. It's the old slash-and-burn technique. Then, if it gets out of control, who gives a shit? It's only forest. This one just happened to be from cooking fish.'

Oblivious to what was happening near Xixuaú, Clark and his Italian film friends travelled back up the Jauaperi on 10 January. By then, the fire had been burning for nearly five weeks and they sailed into a cloud of smoke about 30 kilometres south of Xixuaú. 'You couldn't see anything. You couldn't breathe. We got here to Xixuaú—there was smoke everywhere. And we were like, "What the fuck is going on?"' Clark was furious. No one in the community seemed concerned. No one had done anything, and nor did they plan to.

Clark launched into action, alerting the authorities in Novo Airão, and pleading with those in Manaus to send fire brigades by air and by river. They posted footage of the inferno on Facebook. They got the Brazilian environment ministry involved, so widespread was the destruction. Two weeks after Clark returned, seven weeks after the fire had begun, the authorities sent two aerial water bombers to survey the scene, but even they were helpless. The fire was well beyond the powers of traditional firefighting and entirely beyond control. It would just have to burn itself out.

Then the fire crossed the river. First, an island in the Jauaperi caught fire. Then it leaped to the west bank of the Jauaperi. All of a sudden, the fire went from an environmental catastrophe to an existential threat to the community of Xixuaú itself. Clark and the Italian film crew began to evacuate the women and children. They couldn't take any chances. 'The whole village was going to burn down. It was a *monster*.' Clark barely had time to think. He surely knew that this could be the end of everything, the moment when all of his hard work went to ruin. It could be the moment when nothing else mattered because there would be nothing left to save anyway. More immediately, they had to get everyone out alive.

On 26 January, with fire at the gates of Xixuaú, it began to rain. Not just any rain, but a deluge the like of which hadn't been seen at Xixuaú in years. It rained all day on the 26th. The rain continued without pause all through the 27th. By 28 January, the fire was out. Xixuaú was safe for now.

# 15

# Victory

*2018*

There comes a time in any grand project when it suddenly dawns on those involved that it may not happen after all. By 2018, Clark and his companions had been fighting for Xixuaú to be turned into a reserve for so long that the struggle had become almost an end in itself. Some had fallen by the wayside. Erik Falk died of cancer in 2015. Another of the rocks in Clark's life—Anna Bonari's father Oliviero—had also died. Daniel Garibotti, Tom Haycraft, even Plinho were no longer involved. Anna Bonari came to Xixuaú from time to time for a visit, but she was now a peripheral figure in the Xixuaú story. Clark was back on speaking terms with his brother Paul, even if they were now essentially pursuing different paths. Up among the Waimiri-Atroari, José Porfírio Fontenele de Carvalho died in 2017. In the same year, Clark's father Colin passed away as well. Although he never admitted it—neither to me, nor to anyone else—Chris Clark must have been wondering whether he would live to see the reserve come into being. If there was to one day be a reserve at Xixuaú, perhaps it would fall to the next generation to make it happen.

Xixuaú and the surrounding rainforest remained remarkably intact, despite the fires. Clark knew that, more than anything else, Xixuaú's remoteness had kept it safe. 'Out here, there's no reason to build roads. There's nothing. There's no production. There are no towns. I mean, what would be the point of a road here? It would just be some kind of political statement to destroy the forest. It would be of no practical use.' He also knew that this would not last forever. Parts of the Amazon that had once seemed remote had long ago been cleared.

There had been lots of false dawns at Xixuaú. 'For the last five or six years, we'd been hearing every year: our reserve is going to be created, our reserve is going to be created,' Clark told me in July 2018. 'Every year—disappointment. It never happened. Most of the people thought it was never going to happen.'

And then, all of a sudden, it did.

Early in 2018, Clark's contacts in Brasília told Clark that something might be about to change. Clark was hopeful but didn't take them too seriously. He'd heard such rumours before and they'd always come to nothing. Then, on 5 June 2018, president Michel Temer signed into law the Reserva Extrativista Baixo Rio Branco-Jauaperi. Where once they had hoped for 70,000 hectares (700 square kilometres) around Xixuaú and the Xiparina, the Extractive Reserve of the Lower Rio Branco and Jauaperi came in at 581,173 hectares (5811 square kilometres).

That's almost two and a half times the size of the Australian Capital Territory. The Amazon region is roughly the size of the United States. In that context, locking away Xixuaú is like protecting the state of Delaware as a national park.

'When we started this, when we went to IBAMA in 2000, our request was to protect an area around the Xixuaú,' Clark told me, shaking his head at the wonder of it all. 'The Xixuaú is this river, it's just a little tributary that flows into the Jauaperi.' Instead, the new reserve stretched from the boundaries of the Terra Indígena Waimiri-Atroari, straddled both banks of the Jauaperi, and extended all the way down to the north bank of the Negro. 'We never imagined we'd get all the way to the Rio Negro,' Clark said. 'It's gone way beyond what I hoped for.'

He said this as we sat drinking a celebratory caipirinha on his simple wooden deck at Xixuaú. Barely six weeks had passed since the decree was signed and here we were, looking out at the forest in Brazil's newest protected area. With mock ceremony and no little pleasure, he pulled from a sheaf of papers a copy of *Decreto No. 9.401, de 5 de Junho 2018* (Decree No. 9401 of 5 June 2018). There it was. The reserve that Clark had first imagined 28 years earlier was law. No one could take it away from him and the people of Xixuaú, and from everyone who had been involved in the struggle.

'It's my life's dream and it's come true,' said Clark, shaking his head almost in disbelief. 'It's what I set out to do all those years ago.'

That it was President Temer who gave the reserve its legal imprimatur was more than a little surprising. Under Temer's stewardship, deforestation accelerated in the Amazon by

16 per cent in 2017 alone. In March of that year, just fifteen months before he signed the Xixuaú decree, Temer restructured FUNAI, abolishing nearly one-tenth of its staff positions. He also slashed the environment ministry's budget in half. Commentators referred to Temer's government as 'the agribusiness-friendly Temer administration'.

Clark shook his head again as he spoke of Temer. 'The rate of rainforest destruction is rising again. It went down under the Lula government, and now it's rising again. Temer wanted to take off a hell of a lot of controls. It's so ironic that Temer was the president that signed this reserve.'

As ever with Clark, there was a story involved. Unlike most of Clark's stories, this one was based very much on hearsay. The key to what happened might lie, Clark suggested, in Temer's record low popularity levels—as low as 9 per cent, according to one poll. 'Lula's government was our great hope that it would happen, but then he turned into a total disappointment,' Clark began. 'It makes you want to believe the Gisele Bündchen story . . .' Clark let it hang in the air for a moment, enjoying my puzzled look before continuing. 'We heard that Temer's wife is friends with Gisele Bündchen, the Brazilian model. She's an activist for the Amazon, and so we heard that she approached Temer's wife and said, "Ask your husband to sign a decree creating a nature reserve in the Amazon." Because Temer was leaving and he didn't give a shit, he signed the decree.'

Clark stood up. 'I have no idea whether or not any of that is true,' he said finally. Then he disappeared into the kitchen to pour me another caipirinha, laughing as he went.

~

When Ben Fogle arrived a couple of months after I was with Clark to film an episode of *New Lives in the Wild* for the UK's Channel 5, he asked Clark if Xixuaú was Clark's utopia. 'It's somewhere that in a way is a bit of a utopia, but it's become a reality. So, it's a dream come true more than a utopia. It's a project that I've worked on very, very hard. I and many other people have suffered a lot to get this done. It's been a long, hard struggle, but we've done it, so it's a dream come true.'

It wasn't just that the reserve had happened. Clark could still scarcely believe *how* they had made it happen. 'Nobody has ever created an association, put the local people into the association as joint owners of a larger area with the intention of turning it into a protected nature reserve. Nobody has ever done it before and nobody has ever done it since. It got us into all sorts of trouble because it was like "the gringo association wants to take over the Amazon", and so on. They tried and tried and tried for many years to tear it apart and break it, and they couldn't. In the end, it worked.'

At a micro level, the reserve covered a handful of villages, had a human population of barely 500 and protected a whole lot of rainforest. It took in Xixuaú. It included Gaspar, the small village where Valdemar, and Clark's brother Paul, lived. And it included São Pedro, whose elders had first approached Clark way back in 1990.

But the significance of the reserve extended far beyond its own boundaries. Xixuaú was, Clark said, the final piece of a puzzle. Joining the Jaú and Anavilhanas national parks, the Yanomami and Waimiri-Atroari indigenous reserves, and a patchwork of other reserves, forests and parks, the Reserva

Extrativista Baixo Rio Branco-Jauaperi, with Xixuaú at its heart, completed a mosaic of protected areas, a vast and unbroken expanse of rainforest in the northern Amazon that provides corridors for wildlife and offers protection for future generations. Thanks to Xixuaú, if you knew where to go, you could walk through Brazil from the border of Peru all the way to Brazil's frontier with Guyana without once leaving protected areas. Only rivers would block your path.

With the reserve in place, Clark was excited but impatient. Almost as soon as the news came through, he was looking to the future. On 8 June, he posted on the reserve's Facebook page: 'We have a great opportunity here now. This is going to open a lot of doors. A lot of projects that were on standby until the area was officially declared a reserve can now be reactivated.'

Six weeks later, he was still dreaming. 'I'd like to make this a model for conservation in the Amazon, which means working on a whole bunch of different aspects, like getting payments for environmental services, a carbon credit project, sustainable tourism, sustainable sport fishing, scientific research, scientific training of the local people. We did a project, supposed to be ongoing, with Kew Gardens of London and the National Institute for Amazonian Research (INPA), and they were training some local people here, particularly a couple of young lads from here, to be something like para-botanists to identify different species of plant, to be able to know how to collect and identify those species. That's the sort of job I could see for the people from this area for the future.'

Clark had already spoken with REDD+, a UN program, about a carbon credit payment system: 'We can get a couple of million reais a year coming into here to pay for our projects.' Clark was also convinced that Xixuaú's troubles were over, and that the environment ministry would follow through with enforcement. 'This presence is going to start happening soon. Absolutely. And when it becomes properly organised, we could hopefully have a permanent presence of the environment police in this area. What we'd really like is a floating check-point at the mouth of the Jauaperi River, so that nobody can come in or get out without being checked.'

Wasn't it possible, I wondered, that, having declared the reserve, the government could just forget about it?

'No, no, no. There's going to be a person nominated as respon-sible for this reserve. That will be our direct contact. Then there will be a commission created, and the Indians are going to be involved with this as well. It even says that in the decree. Every community will have a representative on this commission, and it's all about running the reserve and environmental conser-vation, and sustainable development projects, and what you can and can't do in the reserve. The government of Amazonas will be involved. The government of Roraima will be involved. The environment ministry, IBAMA, the Indians, all the local people, some of the World Wildlife Fund [the Amazon Regional Protection Program] will all be involved.'

Yes, there was still opposition, Clark told Ben Fogle just weeks after my visit. 'With the creation of the new reserve, there is going to be a slight increase in the conflict, but then it's going to naturally die down, because people will have to obey the rule of law. That's what's missing here. I'm confident that this is going to start happening soon.'

Whether Clark was as sure as he sounded, I'll never know. His faith in the Brazilian authorities seemed a little unrealistic. Perhaps he was still flush with excitement, and who could blame him after nearly 30 years of struggle? Maybe it was one of his blind spots, taking at face value good news from those about whom others were more wary. It's also possible that he knew deep down that it would not be that simple. Perhaps he just wanted to enjoy the idea for a while.

'In a way, now, it's the beginning of everything,' he told me. 'Now the biggest fight is coming, the biggest challenge is to make it work. It was a victorious first step. There's a lot to do.'

If I were to return three years from now, I asked him, what would I find?

'The government's got itself organised and has taken control, the cooperative has disintegrated, and there will be a *new* organisation comprised of all the inhabitants of the new reserve. Every village will be represented, there'll be government representation, the Indians will be a part of it. So that will then become like the umbrella organisation. And meanwhile, in every small area, I will continue here to do my projects.'

*And in twenty years?* Ben Fogle asked after a successful afternoon of fishing. *What would we find?*

'A happy, united community again and everybody living well. An abundance of wildlife. And even easier fishing than we had this time.'

Clark had carried the idea this far, often through sheer force of will. Why wouldn't he pull off the next stage just as effectively?

# 16

# Local Trouble

*2018*

Six weeks before I arrived in Xixuaú, the reserve became law. Five days before my arrival, Agostinho crossed the water and threatened to kill Clark.

As I wrote in the prologue, all I knew when I arrived in Brazil was that the reserve had been recently decreed into existence. Over the days that followed in Xixuaú, Clark took me back through the story of his life. As we spoke, he carried me along on the journey that took him from Glasgow to Xixuaú, and took the reserve from just another patch of river and rainforest to one of the last reserves to be locked away in the Brazilian Amazon before President Jair Bolsonaro won elections in 2018. For whole days and nights, we sat and talked and drank as the story unfolded. It was only towards the end of my time in Xixuaú that he told me of Agostinho.

Two nights before we were due to return downriver, Clark

took me back to the night of my arrival, and asked me if I remembered hearing a shouted voice from across the lagoon as Valdemar and I explored in a canoe through the darkness. Perhaps. Not really. If I did, I probably thought it was just a noise from the village.

'That was Agostinho,' Clark said. 'He swore. He was yelling at Valdemar: "Don't shine your fucking torch over here!" I don't know what the hell he was doing. He was up to something, something illegal.'

Agostinho knew it was Valdemar?

'He knew.'

I began to feel a little uneasy.

Clark told me how, five days before my arrival, Agostinho had crossed from the village to Clark's hut, where he threatened to kill Clark and burn his hut to the ground, and smashed Clark's canoe before storming off. Clark remained convinced that if Mariana, his cook and family friend, had not been there, things would have been much worse. 'The only reason that he didn't burn the house down was because she refused to leave.'

But why?

'I was his benefactor for fifteen years, and I'm not his benefactor any more. He hasn't got another benefactor, so he's fucked.'

Drugs and alcohol played a part, Clark said, and this made Clark's life much more dangerous. There was, he said, a lot more of a drug problem in remote communities in the Amazon, especially here at Xixuaú, than there ever had been in the past. 'Some of them are out of their heads on drugs—crack, usually. I can see some of the people here, the effect it has on them—they really do lose their minds.'

Clark reminded me that before 2009, the threats had come from outside Xixuaú, from politicians and their hired killers. Most of those threats had been tied to particular events or interests. They had a certain predictable logic. When these threats petered out, the terrain shifted. Since then, any danger to Clark was far more likely to come from within Xixuaú, from amateurs with a personal grievance or vendetta. That these amateurs might also be drunk or high on drugs was far more frightening to Clark than any threat posed by professional killers. These new threats might appear at any time. A drinking session spiralling out of control is all it would take. Everything could change without warning.

Clark almost seemed nostalgic for the days of Francisco and his threats and commissions of inquiry. In fact, Clark had, in the days before my arrival, notified Francisco of Agostinho's threat, and the politician had promised to help in any way that he could. Francisco had even backed Clark's complaint to the police in Novo Airão, to make sure that the police took it seriously. 'He knows these people very well. He knows what Agostinho is like. Francisco said to me, "This guy's going to be leaving here in handcuffs."' Clark also credited Francisco with organising a new internet connection for the village in recent years. Say what you like about Francisco, Clark said, 'but he's still our local representative. Over all these years, 1996 to 2018—that's 22 years—he's the only local politician who has ever regularly been here, who has in any way tried to help.'

Inevitably, there was more to it than Clark saying no to Agostinho. And there was more to it even than the drugs and alcohol. In recent days, Clark had learned that Agostinho had been telling anyone who would listen that Clark had denounced him to the authorities, an accusation Clark denied. In April, a delegation from IBAMA visited Xixuaú. 'They go out and close illegal logging operations or goldmines or catch people hunting turtles. And they came up here. I wasn't even here. I was on my way down to Novo Airão when I bumped into them. We had a chat on the river as they were on their way up. But I didn't say anything about anybody.

'They came up here and they came to Xixuaú. Agostinho was really stupid. He had all these turtle-fishing nets out in the river. IBAMA left. They hadn't found anything untoward here. And after around ten minutes, Agostinho called another guy from the village and they went off to check his nets. On their way out, IBAMA had found the nets and were waiting for him. They brought him back in here and took all his documents. He got caught. They confiscated his nets. And he has got it into his head that it was me who denounced him, and you can't get it out of his head. I've never denounced anyone for this. But now a whole bunch of people who are involved in this are 100 per cent convinced that I am denouncing this activity to the authorities here. And in a way, I'm sort of gratified by that—it's what I should be doing.'

Months had passed since IBAMA's visit, but it's not difficult to imagine a scenario where Agostinho felt spurred to act. He was in trouble with the authorities. Business was bad. And Clark no longer gave him money. One night, drinking with his friends, his anger suddenly began to boil. Perhaps the threat dissipated as he sobered up. But who could say when it might suddenly reignite?

Besides, other things had changed at Xixuaú. Back when things were going well, when the community at Xixuaú was united and everyone had a stake in the success of the project, the locals supported Clark. It was now very different. 'The *vast* majority of people are against the reserve,' Clark said. 'We're fighting the majority. We're in a minority. Their problem now is that the law is going to take over. But that doesn't mean they're going to respect it.'

Valdemar chimed in. 'Most of the villages here are formed by extended families. And most of these families are involved in illegal activities. One will be doing one illegal activity. Another will be doing another illegal activity.'

Locals called it work, said Clark. 'In the beginning, when I first got here, the older guys, the veterans of the river, they lived here, planting their plantations, hunting their meat, catching their fish, eating their turtles. None of them were selling it. That would have been fine in an extractive reserve. But the younger generations don't want to work.' The killing of wildlife now happened on a commercial scale. As Clark saw it, Valdemar's was the last generation to have a sustainable subsistence relationship with the forest. It was almost as if the days of the frontier had returned. Lawlessness and score-settling ruled again.

Despite his success, despite the promise of a new future for Xixuaú and its people, death felt closer for Clark than it had at almost any time in the past 22 years. 'It's not nice for me to have to go to Novo Airão and leave Artemizia and the kids here. She's getting threatened as well. When the kids go to school, they're in the same classroom as Agostinho's kids.

Agostinho could explode if he's just smoked a crack joint. You never know what he might do.'

Artemizia came and sat down at the table. Clark told her that he was telling me about Agostinho. Clearly, they had debated whether to tell me. Valdemar watched his daughter carefully. She sat, grim-faced, for a while. Then she stood up and went down to the balsa platform to stare out across the lagoon.

'I miscalculated. I thought that the new reserve would bring peace and an end,' said Clark. As he said this, I realised that he was less optimistic than he had sounded. He knew very well that the struggle was far from over, and that difficult days could still lie ahead. 'Instead, what's happening is that there's going to be this period of time now between the reserve being decreed by Temer and actually getting organised. What it has brought is a desperation to exploit as quickly as possible and as much as possible before it's too late for these kinds of people. It's raised the ante, rather than lowered the ante.'

Clark was warming to his theme.

'In the old days, all the turtle hunters and commercial fishermen were coming from the outside and we faced them together. And now, all the turtle hunters and commercial fishermen are on the inside. The problem with the mindset of the people here is that they came when everything was already done. They saw it was making money and took over. My family, my friends and I built the school. We built the health post. We put in the internet connection. We started tourism here. They benefited from everything we did. They couldn't survive anywhere else. They don't do any work. They don't do anything. They're just opportunists.'

∾

Clark felt that the matter with Agostinho was now in police hands. As a result of the complaint filed by Clark just before my arrival, all parties had to appear at the police station in Novo Airão at 9 a.m. on 22 August, a few weeks after my visit. Clark would be there. Mariana, too, was planning to attend so she could give evidence. Agostinho would have no choice but to turn up and answer the charges against him. Otherwise, the police would issue a warrant for his arrest.

Out the back of the hut, an increasingly animated family conversation descended into laughter. Valdemar joined them.

'If Agostinho goes to the police station . . .' Clark paused. 'I have a feeling this time he won't because he knows it's going to be much more serious for him. But if he were to turn up at the police station and Mariana is there, he's going to be arrested on the spot. They have no alternative at this point. So he's going to go to prison. Maybe not for that long, but he will go to prison. If he turns up.'

We were silent for a time. I could hear in Clark's voice how weary he was of this never-ending cycle of opposition and threats, and how tired he felt that, even now, he had to watch his back. This conversation would have been unsettling anywhere, but in the Amazon it was even more so. It was about to get even more surreal.

Wasn't Clark worried that Agostinho had backed himself into a corner? And wouldn't that make him even more dangerous?

'If he doesn't turn up, he's just going to try and kill me. At which point it's either him or me. I actually said to the police delegate in Novo Airão, "Look, I have a gun up in Xixuaú, and

I'm going to get another one. If it comes to it, I'm going to have to kill him." And the delegate said, "Look, with everything you've done here, now if you do kill him, don't worry."'

Clark fell silent.

Was he really suggesting that he was prepared to launch a pre-emptive strike?

'Either he's going to be arrested or I'm going to have to kill him.'

I looked at Clark. He held my gaze and he wasn't smiling.

The police and the local authorities had once made his life miserable. Now they were on his side. That in itself was remarkable. Even so, justice in the Amazon has its limits. The police had neither the resources nor the inclination to travel two days upriver to serve the summons on Agostinho. *Would Clark mind passing it on next time he was in Xixuaú?* Clark had little choice but to agree if he wanted to continue with the complaint. It was a reminder, if any were needed, that justice in the Amazon's remote reaches is always an intimate, personal thing. Besides, if matters were to escalate and result in a final, decisive stand-off between the two parties, it would leave the police free to deal with more pressing matters closer to headquarters.

In the whole time that I'd been at Xixuaú, we had never crossed the lagoon to the village. Our failure to do so spoke to Clark's alienation from the community whose huts were visible and whose sounds—a generator, a shouted conversation, someone chopping wood—sometimes carried across the water. There had been so much else to see, so many other conversations to have, that it had never occurred to me to ask if we could visit. All of a sudden, a visit there seemed like a very risky business indeed.

I pressed Clark for clues as to the reception he might expect in the village. Did he go often?

'As often as I have to.'

*Are people friendly?*

'Some are. Others growl when they're near me.'

*So, what do you do normally when you have to go across?*

'I just do it, but there is always the possibility . . . There is an atmosphere of potential violence.'

*Remind me again why we're going.*

Clark handed me the summons. 'Tomorrow when we go over there, I've got to give this to the vice-president of the village, and he has to give it to Agostinho, because I'm not supposed to give it to him personally. Agostinho is going to go crazy. He's going to go *absolutely* crazy. He doesn't even know about it yet.'

What did Clark think would happen—apart, that is, from Agostinho going absolutely crazy?

'There's a chance he'll take some drugs and get drunk or something. We will find out very soon.'

I barely slept that night. I loved hearing the stories of Clark's misadventures, and I took vicarious pleasure in hearing of the dangers he had faced down through the years. Yet I had no desire to put myself in danger. I could understand what had happened to him. I didn't need to experience it first-hand in order to be able to tell his story.

But now I was a part of the story. I was a bystander impli-
cated by my proximity to Clark. I wouldn't be a target. But
anyone who has read tales from the Wild West knows that
no one is safe from the crossfire when the shooting starts. If
Clark crossed to the village, I couldn't stay alone in his hut.
What if Agostinho came looking for Clark and found me there
instead? I'm not sure I could be as brave as Mariana. And what
if something happened to Clark and I wasn't there to witness
it? Any story I told of events as they unfolded would be both
second-hand and a coward's tale. No, I would have to go with
him. But I was frightened.

The next morning, I busied myself with writing notes,
reorganising my backpack, playing hide-and-seek with
Shenaya—anything to take my mind off the visit to the village.
Clark and the others seemed to be in no great hurry.

Clark passed most of the morning in serious conversation
with Valdemar and Artemizia. He didn't offer to translate, and
nor did I ask him to. It didn't help my state of mind when I saw
Clark taking his rifle down the stairs to the boat. 'You never
can be too careful,' he said, trying to laugh it off when he saw
me watching. Clark seemed calm. By the time we were ready to
leave, my nerves were shot.

When it came time to go, my fear had dulled, replaced by
a mixture of disbelief, an awareness of the surreal and, yes, a
little excitement. We were walking into a situation that seemed
scarcely believable. We were two days from the nearest road,
let alone the nearest police station, and here we were hand-
delivering a police summons to the man who had threatened
to kill the man I would be walking alongside. That the accused

was highly unpredictable and might be strung out on alcohol or drugs only added to the apparent lunacy of what we were about to do. We crossed the lagoon in silence.

We pulled up at the riverbank alongside the schoolhouse. It seemed likely that most of the people who lived here knew the nature of our business, or at least of the feud between Clark and Agostinho. People turned their heads to look. Others sat on their doorsteps and watched us arrive, their faces unreadable. Xixuaú the village was a ramshackle, degraded place that carried a hint of Amazonian beauty, like some old beauty dressed in rags in a forgotten corner of the forest. Plank-walled huts on low stilts, some with thatched roofs; a large satellite dish; yellow-and-green macaws screeching in the buriti palms high above the schoolteacher's house—here was a forgotten world of perhaps 30 souls, of blood feuds and lives drifting aimlessly a world away from civilisation.

Clark sat on the stoop of a derelict house and spoke quietly with a handful of locals. I tried the satellite phone and reached home, but all it did was reinforce for me the distance between my life back home and where I found myself now. I told them I was fine and cut the conversation short. Shenaya did cartwheels across the village green.

In time, the vice-president of the village association emerged from the forest at the far end of the village, from the direction of Agostinho's house. Clark rose to meet him. Clark handed over the summons. The vice-president nodded gravely. They shook hands and I followed Clark and the others back to the boat. We pulled away from the riverbank.

It felt like a reprieve but it was a temporary one. We found out that sometime between my arrival in the area and our visit just now to the village, Agostinho had travelled downriver to one of the villages with a friend. The friend had since returned, but Agostinho had disappeared. 'It's strange that he hasn't been in the village,' said Clark as we arrived back at his hut. 'It's strange that he's not here. He doesn't do any work anywhere else. Nobody knows for sure where he is.'

Later in the evening, Clark received a warning. Our time at Xixuaú was nearly over, and we were leaving back downriver in the morning as I made my way home. Details were few, but speculation was rife among those whom Clark considered friends in the village that Agostinho knew of our plans to return to Novo Airão. He was, they said, lying in wait by the riverbank. It would be an ambush, they said, a shot from the cover of trees at a point where Clark would be close to shore.

We were all silent as the news sank in.

'Are you afraid?' I asked.

'Not really, no. I'm sick and tired of it. I've been analysing over the last few days how I think I might feel if I actually did kill him. It's enough. For them'—he nodded towards Shenaya and Raí—'and for Artemizia, it's just not acceptable.'

Thinking about it all later, I was reminded of a conversation Clark had with Ben Fogle in *New Lives in the Wild*.

'Have you saved the Amazon,' Fogle asked, 'or has the Amazon saved you?'

'I think it's more of a love affair,' Clark replied. 'You don't want your love to be harmed, and your love doesn't want you to be harmed.'

'You've done your bit to protect her. Is she going to protect you?' Fogle asked.

'I hope so. You never know, though, with lovers, do you? You can always be betrayed.' Clark laughed. 'We'll see.'

Clark, Valdemar and Artemizia stayed up talking well into the night. I bade them goodnight and paddled the canoe across to my hut, there to lie in bed listening to the night sounds of the Amazon until long after all human voices had fallen silent.

The day dawned, filled with foreboding. Clouds hung low over the forest, and a chorus of red howler monkeys moaned through the trees from somewhere far out across the forest. It was difficult not to feel afraid.

I lay there for a while and listened to the forest waking. I have been in dangerous situations before, but in most cases I only knew of the danger after the event. This was the first morning of my life when I rose knowing that this day could be my last. Clark had known many such mornings. How had he stayed sane? No doubt the first time was always the worst. And unlike Clark, who chose to remain and to stare down the threats many times down through the years, my being here involved no great courage. I had no choice. I hadn't known of the danger until after I arrived. It was not like I could leave by a different route, even if I wanted to. Would I have come to Xixuaú had I known the dangers that lay ahead? I think so, but I cannot say for sure. I don't know.

Clark was keen to get underway, and we left with little fuss.

Artemizia watched us go, her arm around Shenaya. Clark stood tall in the back of the boat, and after a cursory wave, he didn't look back. Valdemar sat in the front, on the lookout, in plain view. I lay down for a short while, but I felt both cowardly and absurd, and I soon sat up. It seemed like the right thing to do. If Clark disagreed, he didn't say so. I braced for a rifle crack and scanned the riverbanks for anything suspicious. But I saw and heard nothing.

No one spoke the whole way downriver.

I was to leave Novo Airão for Manaus the next day. On the morning of my departure, Clark drove me around town in his decrepit car—you could see the road through the floor, and I had to climb into the passenger seat through the window. At one point, he stopped suddenly in the middle of one of Novo Airão's main roads. He had seen the man he was looking for. Clark rushed to the footpath and handed over a large wad of cash. He would have his revolver by the end of tomorrow.

'Do you think you'll survive all this?' I asked.

'Yeah, I do. I'm optimistic. Let 'em come for me. I've got a tough wife and an Indian family. I'll load up my guns. There's so much to do now and so many new projects to develop. I need some peace. And if that involves killing him, then . . .' He didn't need to finish the sentence.

We said our goodbyes. He looked happy. Things were looking up.

I never saw Clark alive again.

# Book Three

# 17

# Bolsonaro's Brazil

*2018–2020*

I left Novo Airão and, soon after, Brazil. Clark and I kept in contact. At first, I half-expected to hear news of a final showdown between Clark and Agostinho somewhere along a remote road, river or forest trail. I worried when I didn't hear from him. Whenever Clark's messages arrived, I read them quickly to make sure that all was well. Then I reread them more slowly. Clark remained unflappable. In time, the threat from Agostinho receded, as so many threats to Clark had in the past.

But threats in the Amazon come in many different guises. On 22 July 2018, the day I arrived in Xixuaú, Brazil's Partido Social Liberal (Social Liberal Party, or PSL) nominated Jair Bolsonaro as its candidate for president. A firebrand Rio de Janeiro congressman, Bolsonaro had always been a far-right populist in the mould of Donald Trump. Some in the international press even called him 'the Trump of the Tropics' or 'the Latin Trump'.

Bolsonaro didn't appear from nowhere. The Workers' Party of presidents Lula and Rousseff had ruled Brazil from 2003 to 2016 and, despite many achievements, their administrations had become mired in corruption scandals in their later years. President Temer (2016–18) faced similar accusations. Bolsonaro rose to prominence just as the government's popularity was at an all-time low, and he tapped into the rampant disaffection Brazilian voters felt towards their political class.

On 28 October 2018, Jair Bolsonaro won the presidency with 55 per cent of the popular vote. Pará, which includes Belém and Santarém, voted for Fernando Haddad of the Workers' Party. But Bolsonaro overwhelmingly carried all other states of the Amazon, including Amazonas, Roraima, Acre and Rondônia. In some areas, he won more than 70 per cent of the vote. Frontier societies are naturally conservative. In the Amazon, Bolsonaro's dismay at the supposed power wielded by indigenous people struck a chord with many *caboclos*. They resented how much land the Indians controlled. Many *caboclos* saw themselves as pioneers and complained about the restrictions that indigenous rights placed on their access to parts of the forest. They hated anyone telling them that they couldn't mine or fish or hunt where they wished. Those who lived in the Amazon's cities, those who knew nothing about the forest and feared it as a result, often shared these views.

Clark wasn't surprised by Bolsonaro's rise. He had foreseen something like this long before the rest of us. As early as 2008, he wrote in his journal that 'Brazil is drifting to the right. Hard times are coming for conservation and sustainable development.' He also knew that many people, even those in Xixuaú, hated the Indians. When the Brazilian navy had stormed up the Jauaperi to take on the Waimiri-Atroari in 2010, many riverbank communities cheered them as they went.

'Most people in the Amazon did vote for him,' Clark told me two years after Bolsonaro swept to power. 'A lot of Brazilians still like him. He speaks to the people quite well, like a man of the people. A lot of people respond to that.'

When he was running for president, Bolsonaro had been clear about his intentions, and he left no doubt as to the sort of president he might become. 'A climate-change denier,' wrote Jon Lee Anderson in *The New Yorker*, Bolsonaro 'came to power with a vehemently anti-environmentalist message, supported by a powerful lobby known as "the three B's": Bibles, bullets, and beef, meaning evangelicals, gun advocates, and the agribusiness industry.' He had many targets, but his views on winding back environmental protections and on indigenous rights in particular blew like a cold wind through those who cared for the Amazon and its people.

Even so, just how far he was willing to go came as a surprise to many. And those who hoped that the office of president might impose some dignity or restraint upon Bolsonaro were quickly disappointed. 'When Bolsonaro was elected, of course everybody was worried,' Clark said. 'But we never realised exactly what it was going to be like until he did actually get in.'

Whatever else you can say about Bolsonaro, he kept many of his promises. Almost from the moment he became president on 1 January 2019, he launched a wide-ranging assault on the Amazon. He called on his supporters to take back the forest, echoing the military's call from the 1940s. At the same time, Bolsonaro slashed IBAMA's budget by a third and gutted the environment ministry's power to prosecute crimes. Where once there had been 1800 IBAMA field agents investigating environmental wrongdoing, there would soon be fewer than 800. Under Bolsonaro, the power to create nature reserves shifted from the environment ministry to the agriculture ministry. The new agriculture minister, the one with the power to make new reserves, was Tereza Cristina Dias. Before becoming minister, she led the congressional farm caucus that was a major voice for agribusiness interests, which were often diametrically opposed to pro-environment and pro-indigenous policies, in the parliament.

In June 2019, six months after Bolsonaro took office, Brazil's National Institute for Space Research (INPE) announced that rainforest destruction had surged by 88 per cent in the past year. Far from trying to stop the devastation, Bolsonaro started calling himself 'Captain Chainsaw'. Two months after INPE's initial report, on 29 August, the same agency told the world that 80,000 wildfires, calculated using detailed satellite images, were blazing across Brazil. More than half of these were in the Amazon. This was, they said, 77 per cent more fires than during the same period in 2018. Others spoke of a 200 per cent increase, and clearing the forest for agriculture and for cattle-grazing were the major causes. This news was too much for Bolsonaro. Accusing INPE of using the fires for political purposes and publishing fake data, Bolsonaro fired the respected physicist Ricardo Magnus Osório Galvão from his position as director-general of INPE. Far from accepting responsibility, Brazil's president said that NGOs had started the fires.

The Amazon was burning, and there was nothing anyone could do to stop it.

In August 2019, a year after I left Xixuaú, Clark wrote to tell me that a team from the Chico Mendes Institute for Biodiversity Conservation would be visiting Xixuaú at the end of September and into October. The institute operates within the environment ministry and is the agency responsible for managing Brazil's protected areas. The Institute was also responsible for preparing a management plan for the reserve. Until this management plan was in place, the reserve remained in limbo, a protected area in name only. Once such a plan existed, everything else—from external funding through to carbon credits and enforcement—became possible. It was an important visit. In spite of everything, Clark was hopeful.

After their visit, Clark sounded as dispirited as I could remember him.

'How did it go?' I asked.

'Their hands are tied. They can't do very much. They're not very efficient.'

Is that because of Bolsonaro? Or was it like that anyway?

'They were never that efficient. But it's because of Bolsonaro that their hands are tied.'

I pushed him for more details.

'It was useless. Basically, they came and said, "The reserve has been made and now we run this area. The rules are this, this, this and this. Nobody has to obey them." So, it was just pretty useless. What the environment ministry does is turn up every few years and start completely from scratch. It turns up talking to the local people as if they have no idea about the environment, and starting an education process all over again. They don't seem to understand that we've been doing this for 30 years.'

I asked if he had been able to talk with any of the people from the ministry. Were there any good guys?

'Some at the top. Not the ones that come to the river. They know nothing about anything. They basically say, "If there are people killing everything and hunting turtles, sooner or later we'll teach them not to." We've been teaching them this for 30 years!'

'Did you expect more, or were you expecting this?' I asked.

'More or less this, I'm afraid.'

No wonder Clark was despondent: these were the same people who would be leading the process of preparing a management plan.

'That's going to take *forever*. And it's all bureaucracy. It's all about passing out jobs to friends and colleagues, and calculations of fish stocks and wood stocks, things like that.'

'It's a long time since I've heard you so pessimistic,' I said.

'There aren't that many optimistic signs here at the moment.'

International leaders tried everything to halt the devastation of the Amazon during Bolsonaro's first year in office. Some expressed concern. Others preferred quiet diplomacy. Others still were less diplomatic and, increasingly desperate, resorted to outright criticism. Nothing worked.

As Clark had discovered back in the late 1990s, foreign interest in the Amazon only stoked the indignation of Brazil's nationalist politicians. When pushed during Bolsonaro's first year, many of his supporters fell back on old catchphrases and enemies. One Bolsonaro advisor named Dom Bertrand de Orléans e Bragança likened the environmental movement to a communist insurgency. 'Greens are the new Reds,' he told Jon Lee Anderson of *The New Yorker*.

Bolsonaro himself pointed out that it was a little rich for European leaders to be lecturing him on protecting the forests when they had destroyed their own. (Coming from almost anyone else, it would be a fair point.) He told those same leaders to mind their own business. Brazil has protected more rainforest than anyone, he said. 'No country in the world has the moral right to talk about Amazon.'

On 23 August 2019, French president Emmanuel Macron tweeted, 'Our house is burning. Literally. The Amazon rain forest—the lungs which produces 20% of our planet's oxygen— is on fire. It is an international crisis.'

Bolsonaro was furious. He accused Macron of 'exploiting an internal issue in Brazil and other Amazonian countries for personal political gains' and of displaying 'a misplaced colonialist mentality in the 21st century'. Bolsonaro threatened to boycott French-made Bic pens. Brazil's popular press and Bolsonaro supporters were just as angry, and Brazil's president did nothing to rein them in. One Bolsonaro supporter posted on Facebook a picture comparing the appearance of Brigitte Macron, 65, with that of Bolsonaro's 38-year-old wife, Michelle. The caption read, 'Now you understand why Macron is persecuting Bolsonaro?' Bolsonaro personally replied on Facebook: 'Do not humiliate the guy, ha ha.' Macron described the comments as 'extraordinarily rude'. In response, Renzo Gracie, a Bolsonaro appointee as tourism ambassador and one-time mixed martial artist, made a public statement addressed to Macron: 'The only fire going on is the fire inside Brazilian hearts and our president's heart, you clown. Come over here, you'll be caught by the neck, that chicken neck. You don't fool me.'

By January 2020, Bolsonaro was an expert at two things: playing to his base and destroying the Amazon. Deforestation during the first year of Bolsonaro's term rose by 85 per cent.

Bolsonaro and his administration were not uniquely responsible for the destruction of the Amazon rainforest. It had been going on since the 1960s and, by the time Bolsonaro came to power, it had been in a state of increasing peril for more than half a century. What Bolsonaro did was accelerate the process and, as a result, the Amazon rainforest and its ecosystems are now closer than ever to what's known as the tipping point.

The tipping point is the moment when the fundamental scale and character of the Amazon changes. It's when enough of the rainforest disappears for the balance to tip from rainforest to savannah, or open grasslands, across a wide enough area. It's when the Amazon's role in world weather systems changes, when it no longer produces its own rainfall. It's when the Amazon begins to emit more carbon than it absorbs.

No one really knows exactly where the tipping point lies. Most scientists agree that we will reach the tipping point when 25 to 30 per cent of the rainforest has disappeared. Those same experts generally agree that 17–20 per cent has already gone, and that we have between 15 and 30 years of unchecked deforestation before we arrive at the tipping point. But the science surrounding this is notoriously inexact.

A 2020 study published in *Nature Communications* found that, based on rainfall levels, 40 per cent of the Amazon could already be functioning in the same way as does a savannah. While that wouldn't push us over the threshold immediately, it would bring us closer to the point of no return much sooner. It should be obvious why studies like this matter. Twenty per cent of the world's oxygen comes from the Amazon. The Amazon's trees store up to 120 billion tonnes of carbon dioxide. And the process of unravelling is so much faster than the process of carbon capture. As Andrew Revkin wrote, 'An atom of carbon that had been locked up in a tree trunk for perhaps a century, once liberated as pure carbon soot, took just ten days to travel from the tropics to the South Pole.'

At the height of the Brazilian wildfires in August 2019, the skies turned dark over São Paulo from all the smoke. Events like this were, Clark had told me a year earlier, a dramatic vision of a much darker future. 'If it gets beyond the tipping point, then there's no point even worrying about saving the rest of it. If the Amazon gets to the point of not being able to regenerate, and not being able to survive anymore, and not creating the rainfall, the whole area is going to be compromised. You're talking about the vast majority of the population of Brazil starving. When it gets beyond another few per cent of Amazon rainforest destruction, they're going to have a big wake-up call. Brazil's central-south is going to turn into a desert. And then it's too late. The question of whether we're going to be fucked or whether we're not going to be fucked isn't that far away anymore.'

Bolsonaro's destruction of the rainforest went hand in hand with an assault on indigenous rights. Among his first appointments when he became president had been Damares Alves, an ultra-conservative evangelical minister, to lead FUNAI, Brazil's once-respected indigenous affairs agency. Then Bolsonaro buried FUNAI within the new Ministry of Women, Family and Human Rights.

One of Bolsonaro's biggest public-policy obsessions was to bring the forest's indigenous populations into mainstream Brazilian society. Like Donald Trump, Bolsonaro enjoyed how he could communicate directly with the world, without a filter, on Twitter. He used it to try out ideas. He made major policy announcements on the platform. He couldn't have cared less about any public outcry. Less than a week after taking office, he tweeted that 'Less than one million people live in those places isolated from the real Brazil. They are exploited and manipulated by NGOs. Together let's integrate those citizens and give value to all Brazilians.' On another occasion, he said, 'We can't keep living like poor people on earth that is so rich. We want to include the Indians in our society, and a large part of them want it that way too.' John Hemming, historian of the Amazon, described it as 'the absurd notion that Indians *wanted* to be released from communal societies so that they could prosper as ordinary citizens'. It mattered not at all to Bolsonaro and his supporters that almost every indigenous group in Brazil angrily refuted Bolsonaro's claims.

Long before he was elected, Bolsonaro had said that 'The Indians do not speak our language, they do not have money, they do not have culture. How did they manage to get thirteen percent of the national territory?' Another time, he described the Amazon as 'the richest area of the world' and boasted that 'I'm not getting into this nonsense of defending land for Indians'.

In his first year, Bolsonaro closed two military outposts in Yanomami territory, in Brazil's far north. Ordinarily, indigenous groups would have been happy to see the soldiers leave. But these outposts were there to prevent illegal mining on Indian land. With their removal, the government was making a statement, and those to whom it was directed heard the message. In very little time at all, *The New Yorker* reported, more than 20,000 prospectors—*garimpeiros*—illegally invaded the reserve. When illegal miners killed an indigenous man in his village elsewhere at around the same time, Bolsonaro's environment minister blamed the victim. The Indian, he said, was drunk and had drowned.

For Bolsonaro, the issue of illegal mining was personal. His father had once been an itinerant dentist and had prospected for gold in the Serra Pelada—the mine that had been searingly photographed by Sebastião Salgado. Bolsonaro always spoke of the Serra Pelada with nostalgia. And, anyway, illegal mining in the Amazon was a perfect fit for his world view. In August 2019, he announced that he planned to legalise mining on indigenous land. Two months later, he told a group of miners that, 'Interest in the Amazon isn't about the Indians or the fucking trees—it's about mining.'

Not surprisingly, he soon took aim at the Waimiri-Atroari.

Where environmentalists and indigenous groups saw massacres of the Waimiri-Atroari in the 1970s and 1980s, Brazilians like Bolsonaro saw an essential new road and Indians standing in the way of progress. For many in Roraima in particular, the nightly closure of the BR-174 was an insult. It was, they said, a roadblock to their state's economic advancement. It was an embarrassment. It held the state back. That semi-naked Indians could decide who gets in and out of their state . . . well, that was just an outrage in a modern country like Brazil.

At the end of February 2019, General Otávio do Rêgo Barros, a presidential spokesman, announced that the National Defence Council had approved the long-delayed construction of a transmission line, or powerline, from Manaus to Boa Vista. The reasons behind the decision seemed simple enough. Boa Vista was the only one of Brazil's 26 state capitals not connected to the national electricity grid. Seventy per cent of Roraima's electricity came from neighbouring Venezuela, a country in a near-permanent state of economic and social collapse. And besides, Bolsonaro had called for Venezuelans to overthrow the arch-left regime of their president Nicolás Maduro, so retaliatory measures were always possible. Much of Roraima cheered when the government announced that the project would proceed. Connecting Boa Vista to the rest of Brazil was another way of bringing the state into the national fold.

As ever, it wasn't that simple. A study by the state itself had found that renewable energy sources, such as solar and wind power, would be the more economical path towards energy independence.

Even so, Brazil's government approved the project. The Tucuruí transmission line, as it was called, would shadow the BR-174, including for 122 kilometres through Waimiri-Atroari land. Although the line would eventually run alongside the road, each of the 200 transmission towers required an area of cleared forest equivalent in size to a soccer pitch. Other collateral infrastructure included maintenance and access roads. Crews would need to regularly clear branches from nearby trees. And there would be a dramatic increase in the number of outsiders on the reserve throughout the three years of construction. According to Waimiri-Atroari representatives, 27 of 37 potential environmental and social impacts identified in a project proposal would be irreversible, to say nothing of the fact that the lines would not benefit the Waimiri-Atroari at all. None of the electricity carried across their land would ever reach Waimiri-Atroari villages.

The Waimiri-Atroari saw the Brazilian government's decision to proceed as a declaration of war. That same Brazilian government just didn't care.

General Otávio do Rêgo Barros justified the decision as one of national security. 'The Indians will be consulted,' he said, 'but national interest must prevail.' One of Bolsonaro's minister released a statement that 'The government's dialogue with the indigenous peoples continues but their permission is no longer a condition for the concession of the licence to build.'

The Tucuruí transmission line was a throwback to the days of the pre-1985 military dictatorship. It was also a symbol of the new government's determination to push ahead with large projects on indigenous land, regardless of the opposition. Said Sydney Possuelo, the respected former director of FUNAI, 'The situation of Brazil's indigenous peoples has never been good. But during 42 years of working in the Amazon, this is the most dangerous moment I have seen.'

Clark watched all of this with grim, knowing bemusement. He also understood that he should keep his head down.

'Thank god you got the reserve signed and legal before Bolsonaro got in,' I told him over the phone.

'Yeah, at least that's done and cannot be undone.'

I asked if Bolsonaro could touch the reserve.

'I don't think he's ever heard of it.'

I said I hoped it stayed that way.

'Yeah, because I would be a perfect enemy for him. I tick all the boxes—foreigner, Amazon, ecology, friend of Indians, long hair—everything he hates! He's fighting with the Indians as well.'

But *could* the reserve be undone? It was a question I had often wondered. Surely, a government that decreed certain classes of protected land could also remove those same protections? Clark didn't seem to think so. After all, Brazil's 1988 democratic constitution was quite specific when it came to indigenous rights. The constitution declared the country's indigenous people to be descendants of the first Brazilians. Article 231 then provided that 'Indians shall have their social organization, customs, languages, creeds and traditions recognized, as well as their original rights to the lands they traditionally occupy, it being incumbent upon the Union to demarcate them, protect and ensure respect for all of their property.'

Paragraph 1 of Article 231 clarified that 'Lands traditionally occupied by Indians are those on which they live on a permanent basis, those used for their productive activities, those indispensable to the preservation of the environmental resources necessary for their well-being and for their physical and cultural reproduction, according to their uses, customs and traditions.'

Paragraph 2 went further: 'The lands traditionally occupied by Indians are intended for their permanent possession and they shall have the exclusive usufruct of the riches of the soil, the rivers and the lakes existing therein.' And in case the point was missed, paragraph 4 states that 'the lands referred to in this article are inalienable and indisposable and the rights thereto are not subject to limitation.'

So far so good.

But Paragraph 3 appears to offer an exception. It states that 'hydric resources, including energetic potentials, may only be exploited, and mineral riches in Indian land may only be prospected and mined with the authorization of the National

Congress, after hearing the communities involved, and the participation in the results of such mining shall be ensured to them, as set forth by law.' Forget the legalese. In other words, as long as mineral or hydroelectric rights were somehow involved, the constitutional protections afforded to Indian lands were not absolute. Article 231, Paragraph 6 suggested that the 'relevant public interest of the Union' could override the protections.

It was most likely these provisions that the Bolsonaro administration had in mind when, in April 2019, the president told supporters that he planned to open up the Amazon's Reserva Nacional do Cobre e Associados (RENCA) to mining. Thought to be rich in gold, copper, iron ore and more, the reserve straddles the states of Pará and Amapá. It was a presidential decree that had established the reserve in 1984, so Bolsonaro argued that he, as president, could reverse the decree. The constitutional exceptions were also no doubt behind a law he put before Congress, in August 2019, that sought to legalise mining on indigenous land. Eight months later, he directed FUNAI to authorise the sale of land on 237 indigenous territories.

The only drawback of such laws was that the process of overriding constitutional protections is complicated. In most cases, nothing could happen until Brazil's Supreme Court had ruled on the constitutionality of any such law, and that could take years.

But it wasn't Bolsonaro who found a way around it. It had already been done by his political opponents.

In 2012, then-president Dilma Rousseff was eager to change the image of the Workers' Party. Mired in scandals, the administration wanted to make itself more friendly to business. One way to do this was through large-scale infrastructure projects. It was the era of big dams, and Rousseff chose to take a stand with the São Luiz do Tapajós hydroelectric project, south of Santarém. To gain legal approval she used a little-known measure that no government had used since the end of military rule in 1985. Known as the Suspensão de Segurança (Suspension of Security), the measure allowed for a president to demand that a court overturn lower-court decisions without legal argument. All it had to do was invoke a justification based on national security, public order or national economy. She also used Medidas Provisórias (MPs), interim presidential decrees that required no congressional approval, to reduce the size of relevant protected areas.

As noted earlier in this book, it was the public outcry, rather than any legal limitations, that stalled the São Luiz do Tapajós dam project. But Bolsonaro appeared to take perverse pleasure in thumbing his nose at public opinion. If he decided to deploy these measures, what would stop him?

I never got the chance to put these legal questions to Clark. He probably already knew about them. Either way, the whole situation depressed him. The best-case scenario? That Bolsonaro would be too busy to turn his attention to Xixuaú. Even if that happened, everything that would move the reserve forwards would have to remain on hold until Bolsonaro left office.

'We can't do anything until the management plan for the reserve is made,' he told me early in 2020. 'And the management plan for the reserve seems to be a long, long way away, because it depends on the environment ministry. They are completely handicapped at the moment.'

There were moments in our final conversations when Clark seemed more optimistic.

'You can do a lot of damage and you can do *some* good in four years. But it's not long term. Politics is not long term. Human beings do not think long term. It's the difference between one World Cup and another.'

He stopped talking. A long, hacking cough broke the silence.

'It's a political question. I mean, if the government changes, and we get a more favourable government in for nature, then you could get some financing to do a management plan. Still, it would be heavily in favour of the human inhabitants. But there might be something left over for nature there.'

Mostly, however, Clark was losing hope. He had stared down so many threats and setbacks over the years. There had been moments when any normal, sane person would have given up. He had never wavered. And yet, if Clark was no longer hopeful, what hope was there for the rest of us? I tried to cheer him up. I tried to steer him back to the notion that at least the reserve was locked away and couldn't easily be touched.

'But it is being touched,' he replied gloomily. 'There's a lot of turtle-trafficking going on. There's a lot of commercial fishing going on, even by the local people. And nobody's doing anything to stop it, because there is no law. There are no laws being enforced. There's no direct conservation happening. There was definitely a coordinated move to raze the forest and occupy areas in Brazil. And it's coming from the government.

242

There's impunity. That's what they aimed for and it's what they're giving.'

I didn't like where this conversation was going, but I had to ask: where does this end? Was there any hope that this was a cycle in which Bolsonaro could later get voted out, and then it would swing back the other way?

'I don't think this is only Bolsonaro. The world has become so human oriented. It's all about people. If we save an animal, it's all because we're deciding to be kind and do a favour to it, and give it a little space to live in. It's all in relation to our needs. Do we need this animal? Is it any use to us? Is it pretty? Is it symbolic? If so, maybe we should save it. But if it isn't, fuck it! It's all about humans.'

He paused for a minute to gather his thoughts.

'It was the Wild West here, and it's now gone back to the Wild West. There was a period when it looked like it might be civilising a bit. But it's gone back to being the Wild West again.'

I reminded him that the odds had always been stacked against him, and against Xixuaú, and that still they'd triumphed.

'It's a miracle we got the reserve made,' he agreed.

Was it all in vain? Had too much been lost at Xixuaú?

'In our area, it's still recuperable. Our area is still a wilderness. *Our* area. There's still no commercial logging or land-clearing here. It's too far away, too complicated, too inaccessible. But if you sum it up in other areas, in the south of the Amazon for example, how soon will it be irreversible? I do sometimes wonder if it has all been in vain.'

It was a depressing thought, especially coming from Clark. He had one more for me.

'What I think will happen is that some little pockets will end up being preserved. They won't make any difference in the long run. But they'll try to save some little pockets. There are some wealthy people who will want to be able to come and enjoy a little nature.'

At what point does someone like Clark give up? What was his tipping point? As I spoke with Clark, I couldn't get out of my head something that I had read. It had stuck in my mind as a passage of such poignant, existential sadness that it haunted my thoughts as I tried to imagine a better future for the Amazon. The events in question occurred in the southern Amazonian state of Rondônia. They first appeared in an NGO journal *Cultural Survival Quarterly*, in an article by Italian anthropologist Gilio Brunelli, and were recounted by Andrew Revkin in his 1990 book *The Burning Season*.

'On Monday, August 26, 1985, forty Zoró warriors adorned with red and black dye, macaw and sparrow hawk feather crowns and black necklaces across their breasts, armed themselves with shotguns, bows and arrows, knives and machetes, left the village and disappeared into the bush. They won their first battle and seized three whites who were brought back to the village to be kept as hostages,' wrote Brunelli. They went out again in search of more captives, but three days later returned forlorn, realizing that there were far too many whites already established on their land. They released the prisoners and surrendered to their fate.

In the Brazil of Jair Bolsonaro, it was hard not to see this as a metaphor for the future. If Clark and those like him reached a similar point of surrender, it would all be over.

I put Clark's pessimism down to the darkness of the hour. I clung to the idea that as long as Clark was alive, as long as the Xixuaú remained intact, there was still hope.

After all, there would always be Xixuaú.

# 18

# Death of a Different Kind

## *2020*

On Tuesday, 21 April 2020, I sent an email to Chris Clark. In it, I told him that I was ready, that it was time to start talking in earnest about the book I wanted to write. It was to be about Xixuaú, and about Clark himself, and when could we talk?

The COVID-19 pandemic was taking hold everywhere and the situation in Brazil was particularly uncertain. I assumed and hoped that Clark was in Xixuaú, blissfully remote from a world that was descending very rapidly into a once-in-a-century meltdown. We would go for months with no contact. Then one of us would write and the conversation would resume where it had left off. Usually, Clark responded within hours of any message. But I heard nothing back. I wasn't worried. Perhaps he was offline. Perhaps the connection was down at Xixuaú.

Normally, I would have waited. But my mind had turned to Xixuaú. My previous book was off to the printer and would soon take on a life of its own. There was nothing more I could do. It was time to move on. For months I had known that a whole pile of story ideas was waiting for me. I was aware of their presence, knew I'd get to them when I could, and knew that I'd have to pick one. But—and this is how it always happened—all of a sudden, I knew that Xixuaú was the story I simply had to write. All of a sudden, it couldn't wait.

I checked my email each morning for any sign of Clark. Nothing. I began to panic. What if Agostinho had finally tracked Clark down and killed him? When I didn't hear anything later in the week, I sent him a message via WhatsApp. When I got no reply, I emailed again.

On Saturday 25 April, Clark replied.

*HI Anthony. Yes I am receiving your messages but irony on irony I left XIxuau MOnday and had to go to Manaus ysterday to hospital. I Had a srroke and it seems I have lung cancer which has spread to my brain and I mIght die at any moment. I shoul be in hospital and am looking into the possibility, BUT we are one of the worst hit areas for corona and the hospitals are all full. So i dont know what to sat, Maybe we could talk by whatsapp. BUT my left side is pretty uselees so even writing email is a problem.*

I sat there, reeling. I read it again, hoping I'd misunderstood, and again, knowing that I hadn't. If anything felt familiar in that moment, it was the numb disbelief—the same thing I had felt upon receiving news of my father's rapid deterioration in 2015. It didn't make sense to me. It couldn't be. Not Clark.

I had imagined many scenarios. Most involved hearing that Clark had been attacked or killed or imprisoned, or all of the above. Any of those scenarios would have been perversely believable. All would have been tragic, yet unsurprising ends to a life spent fighting for the Amazon. He would have been martyr to a cause to which he had given his life. But this was just pure, dumb luck. Not like this. Not now.

Clark had contemplated his own death many times in the past. Death, after all, had always been a possibility. As I knew from my last night in Xixuaú, you couldn't start a day wondering if it would be your last and not imagine exactly how it might end, how it might feel, or what it might mean. Listening later to the tapes of our conversations, I realised how often in Xixuaú we spoke about death, especially Clark's. In the course of his life in the Amazon, death was no abstract thing. It was what one spoke about from time to time. It was always possible.

Years before, perhaps around 2008, long before Agostinho, Clark had written in his journal that 'I have become convinced that there is a very good chance I will die at the hands of some young buck out to prove a point. How there is a good chance that I will be removed as a disturbance . . . I'm giving violence and disease a fifty-fifty chance. I sort of think it might not be too far down the line.' Later in the same passage, he wrote, 'I wonder if we will all go out believing that it is too early, and there is still much to be done.'

In 2018, not long after my visit to Xixuaú, Clark told Ben Fogle, 'I belong here now. I'll be buried under some big old tree out the back here.'

Fogle asked whether Clark worried about getting older.

'I think that getting older in a place like this, you have to accept that you're not going to get the level of medical attention that you would get in the First World,' Clark replied. 'So, if you're going to spend the rest of your life in a place like this, it's probably going to be a couple of years shorter than it would be with proper medical attention. But, you know, what the hell.'

'That's a sacrifice you're willing to take?' Fogle asked.

'I'd rather live somewhere where I'm happy than prolong my life somewhere where I'm not happy.'

Even so, this is not how the story was supposed to end.

Those who knew Clark well had known for a while that something was wrong.

'I'd been telling him for the last two years that he needed to see a doctor,' Nicolle told me from Italy. 'His cough was not okay. He was not strong anymore. The last time I've been to Brazil, I told him, "Dad, you're not okay. You have to see a doctor." I couldn't imagine the whole picture. I could tell that something was not okay. Cathleen as well. He wouldn't listen.'

Cathleen and her partner had talked about it, about how Clark seemed to be slowing down. 'We used to think it was something to do with his style of life,' Cathleen told me. 'That, and the fact that, of course, the years were passing. He was almost 60 and he used to carry a lot of heavy stuff, and do those trips up and down the river in that speedboat—sun, rain, coming and going all the time. He never stopped. And always he had a lot of worries. So I thought it was something to do with that.'

In September 2019, Anna Bonari visited Brazil. Cathleen was living and working in Novo Airão, and the trip was also a chance to visit Clark and Xixuaú. It had been Bonari's home for many years, and she hadn't seen Cathleen and her daughter—Bonari's granddaughter—for too long. Bonari would have given anything to return to Brazil to live, but Nicolle was studying at university in Bologna, and Bonari's elderly mother needed constant care. Clark and Bonari got along fine, and each could handle the other in small doses.

Bonari was convinced that something was wrong. 'Chris wasn't well,' she told me a year later. 'He was very slow. He was very silent. I made lasagne. I made gnocchi. I made everything I knew he loved. And then he would ask for a plate of pasta with tomato sauce—a very simple one. I said to Chris "You are not well!" He was different. He was different . . .' Her voice trailed off, as if trying to make sense of it all. 'I kept saying to him for a long, long time, even from Italy: "Chris, go to the doctor. Chris, go to the doctor."'

A few months later, Clark began to notice the changes himself. 'About six months ago, I started feeling a bit weaker,' he told me in late April 2020. 'I started feeling like I had one leg longer than the other. Not unwell. A bit different, like I was getting older. It was like a sort of slow degenerative process.

My balance wasn't good. But I never got the effects of a stroke. I did at the end because I was falling down. It kind of crept up on me slowly.' He wasn't the only one.

In early April, Cathleen was up at Xixuaú, visiting with her daughter. 'It didn't start immediately,' Cathleen remembered. 'He had some confusion, loss of strength in his arms and his legs, but then he just went down, down, down, down every day.' Nicolle, who was still in Italy, later told me how Cathleen had become worried about Clark's health. 'Soon after Cathleen arrived up in Xixuaú, she noticed that he wasn't managing to move properly,' Nicolle remembered. 'That's what she noticed first. He couldn't move one arm. He couldn't talk properly. He was always sleepy. He got confused about things and he would repeat the same things. So, in the end we got scared that it could be something like Alzheimer's.'

Everyone had known that something wasn't right. They had been ignoring it for weeks, even months. They all hoped that it would go away. 'You kind of explain things to yourself in your mind so that they make sense,' said Cathleen. 'And you put them aside. So until I really saw him in Xixuaú, those days that I was there, I didn't realise.'

On Monday 20 April, at about the precise moment that I emailed Clark to tell him that I was ready to tell his story, Clark fell down the stairs outside his hut. Suddenly, they all knew. For Clark, this was his moment of realisation. For Cathleen, realisation dawned, clear and awful, when her father couldn't get back up. Clark was a little reluctant to leave at first. But he knew, and Cathleen didn't have to work too hard to convince him, that they had to leave, and leave now.

The journey downriver was a nightmare. It was the start of the high-water season, a time of flooded forests, of rising rivers and heavy rains. The boat they wanted to take broke down. They couldn't wait to have it fixed, so seven of them piled into a much smaller boat that belonged to Artemizia's grandfather. Apart from being small, the boat wasn't really fit for purpose. It filled with water quickly, and they had to stop often—every hour at least—to bail out the water. There were three young children on board. All of the adults were worried sick about Clark. Heavy rain battered them for much of the journey. It was impossible to stay dry, it was freezing cold, and everyone was cramped and miserable. A journey that should have taken six or so hours took two days and nights. For those on board, it felt like it lasted forever. Clark was never one to complain. 'It was horrible,' he told me.

When I spoke to him on the phone a few days after the hellish trip downriver, he was resting at his daughter's home in Novo Airão, with his family gathered around. By then he had been to Manaus to see a doctor. 'I should be in hospital,' he told me. 'But the hospitals are full there. There's too much coronavirus in Manaus. It's really bad.'

Clark was waiting on test results, and would be returning to Manaus to see an oncologist a few days later. But he had already seen a neurologist, and there seemed to be little doubt about the diagnosis. It wasn't a stroke at all. If anything, it was worse. He had lung cancer and the cancer had spread to his brain, where a massive cerebral oedema was affecting his brain function and, by extension, his coordination. 'It would have been better if I'd had a stroke,' he said. 'At least I would have had some advance warning. It's pretty far advanced, unfortunately.'

The line from Novo Airão wasn't great. He was breaking up.

'I've been abusing myself for a long time,' Clark told me before the line went dead. 'Forty-five years of smoking, more or less.'

A few days later, we spoke again. He had been to an oncologist who confirmed the diagnosis. But hospitals in Manaus were in a state of near-collapse, and the costs of seeing private consultants and seeking treatment in private hospitals were eye-wateringly high. 'Here with this bloody coronavirus, it's a disaster,' he told me. 'It's a bloody disaster.' He decided to fly to the UK, via Frankfurt. A pregnant Cathleen and her daughter would go with him. Once in the UK, he planned to stay with his sister, Regan, and exercise his rights as a citizen to treatment through Britain's National Health Service, the NHS.

Where once we had talked easily about death, the chilling immediacy of the threat to his life gave me pause. There can be something indelicate in trying to get someone to imagine a future in which they will play no part because they will be dead. Clark gave no indication of being uncomfortable with the topic, but we circled around it anyway. As always with him, Clark spoke of death less as an existential threat than an inconvenience.

'Just when we needed to talk, this happens,' he said.

'And here I was thinking it was going to be Agostinho who got you.'

'Agostinho has completely changed—he's found God! He went to Moura, and he went around making fun of some guy.

The next time he went to Moura, this guy's family got hold of him and beat the shit out of him. He ended up in hospital, firstly in Barcelos, then they had to send him to Manaus because he was so badly injured. And now he's found Jesus. So now he's all religious and saying how the devil was inside him, and now he's got the devil out of him. Some preacher has taken him in. He's now doing all these bible messages on Facebook. So that's progress.'

(I learned later from Paul, Clark's brother, that Agostinho had gone to Chris to beg his forgiveness. 'Christopher was delighted,' Paul told me. 'It really did amuse him.')

He was obviously going to be out of action for a while. Was there someone who could take up the reins at Xixuaú?

'Well, yeah, there's Cathleen, there's Valdemar, there are some people. Artemizia. Nicolle also helps. We'll work something out. I've got a good crew, a good bunch of people. We'll muddle through until something changes again. There's still a lot to do, especially with this government.'

Just once, he let his guard slip. It would be the only time I ever heard him admit that he was finding it difficult. 'The only problem for me, Anthony, is that I think I'm not really going to be the boss of my own time and my own life for a while.'

He paused for long seconds.

'It's tough. It's very tough.'

Death came quickly in the end.

Clark said goodbye to Artemizia and Shenaya in Manaus and flew to São Paulo, transited in Frankfurt, and then continued on to London. He must have known that he might be leaving Brazil for the last time, that he might be saying goodbye to his wife and youngest daughter forever. Artemizia was herself unwell and undergoing tests, but they both held it together for the sake of Shenaya. Did he know that he was dying? 'He tried,' Nicolle told me. 'He tried his very best for Shenaya, because she's eight. But he knew it.'

Clark spoke little about that final farewell to his wife and youngest daughter. In fact, he never spoke openly about his second marriage; it was the one area of his life that he kept as a guarded secret. I never learned the reasons for this, and I drew no conclusions from his silence, other than to wonder whether he did it to shield Artemizia and Shenaya from public attention. But it does leave me with questions about his emotional state in his final years, and, unfairly, it casts Artemizia's role in his life into shadow.

He touched down in the UK in the first week of May. He moved in with his sister, Regan, in Camberley, close to London. Nicolle came over from Italy and, together with Cathleen, who was by now five months pregnant, moved in to be with their dad. He registered with the local health authorities. He began seeing doctors. No one was optimistic about his long-term prognosis. But on a day-to-day basis, things were going as well as could be expected. Texting and emailing were difficult for him as he had lost some coordination on his left side, so over the weeks that followed, we spoke often on the phone. He was under no illusions as to the seriousness of his condition. But he was, for the most part, cheerful and back to his old self, excoriating his enemies and speaking about the future. By the end of

May, he had the results of the various tests and biopsies. Soon after, he began treatment.

'He started his chemo,' Nicolle told me later. 'Then we went to hospital in London, and he did his three cycles of radio-therapy. It was brilliant. I mean, he had no consequences at all. He wasn't dizzy, he wasn't losing his hair. We were super happy about the results and we said, "Okay, maybe, you know, every day is a gift. Maybe we can get a little bit more time with you."'

Cathleen was also there, and she felt the same way. 'We were all very optimistic. The doctors were too. Of course, the situation wasn't good right from the beginning. We knew we were dealing with a bad situation. But we imagined that we would have time to get him back to Brazil if it was needed, and to enjoy at least some months, you know? Not years—I don't think so. At least some months.'

A few weeks later, such hopes didn't appear too unrealistic.

*Treatment going well*, he wrote to me in a WhatsApp message on 15 June. *Finished radiotherapy and now getting through chemo. Hopefully home after that.*

On 17 June, Clark was admitted to hospital with back pain. He also had a fever. I wrote to him five days later asking how he was, but received no reply. On 24 June, Nicolle wrote to tell me that the infection was a little better but that he still had pain and fever. By 29 June, I was getting worried and wrote again. His reply came back almost immediately. *hi Anthony. one problem after another keeps cropping up. a mysterious bacteria infection that they. cannot figure out. sort that and I start to bleed for no reason in the intestinal cavity. now investigating that. So in hospital 13 days today wasting time.*

By 1 July, he seemed better, more optimistic, and spoke of being well enough for his next chemo session a week later. On 9 July, I wrote to ask how he was and whether he was out of hospital. Within the hour he replied: *yes i m home. Nicolle can tell you.*

What I didn't know at the time was that on 9 July, doctors told Clark that there was nothing more they could do for him. They gave him the option of leaving hospital to spend his last hours or days with his family. He accepted gladly.

They returned to Regan's house in Camberley. It was not far from where, as a sixteen-year-old, he had fled home to begin a lifetime of adventures. Clark's world had come full circle.

'We talked a lot on the last day,' Nicolle told me later. 'He was fully aware, even under morphine. He never lost control. Never.'

He began to put his affairs in order. Xixuaú would have to take care of itself. He had done all he could. In his final hours, it was family that mattered. He phoned Artemizia and Shenaya to say goodbye. I think of Shenaya. Down a poor phone line came her father's voice, telling her that he wouldn't be coming home, but that he loved her. I think of her receiving the news that her world was about to come tumbling down around her. I can see a bewildered little eight-year-old girl in the Amazon. Photos of Clark and the rest of her family fill her bedroom. Rollerskates hang from her pink walls. A fish mobile dangles from the ceiling. Does she understand that her father will never return to tuck her into bed at night?

And I see Artemizia, the truth suddenly dawning as she learns that she will have to face their complicated world alone.

Clark phoned Anna Bonari. He told her that she would always be the love of his life, which, in spite of everything, she surely was. He called Cathleen, who had had to leave her father's bedside because of her pregnancy, and he told her that she would always be his first princess. He turned to Nicolle and told her how much he adored her.

'We were lying together in the bed, and it was just like falling asleep together,' she remembered. 'He just fell asleep.'

It was the 10th of July. Two months short of his 60th birthday, Christopher Clark was dead.

# Epilogue

## *2022*

How quickly a life unravels. From falling down the stairs in Xixuaú to dying in London had taken only 81 days. Everyone was in shock. It was especially difficult for Cathleen, who was seven months pregnant. Having known that he would never meet his grandson, Clark asked if he could name him. Joshua was born on 8 September.

Clark had friends and family all over the world. But the world was in the midst of a pandemic and only closest family members ever got to say goodbye. Even for them there was no funeral, no wake, no moment where they could all gather around and remember Clark's life.

Over the weeks and months that followed, I spoke often with his family, and we pieced together our own wake of sorts. One of the more poignant observations came from Anna Bonari, and it rang true: 'When I heard he was sick, I said to Chris, "You have to resist because we have to fight for the rest of our lives." I've always thought that one day when I'm older, I'll go back there and I'll be sitting in front of Xixuaú with a caipirinha at five o'clock, fighting with Christopher. And now I'll never be able to do this anymore. And it makes me so angry.'

Clark's mother was, by all accounts heartbroken. In Clark's final days in hospital, Barbara Clark arranged for a priest to visit. Some family members were uneasy with the whole idea. Clark was not at all religious and was clearly uncomfortable at having to endure a priest by his bedside. But he tolerated it because it was important to his mother. Those who knew him best knew that he enjoyed far more the hash cookie that Adrian, Clark's younger brother, smuggled in, or the gin and tonic that Nicolle prepared.

After Clark's death, his mother posted on Facebook: 'When you take him home, Cathleen, Nicky and Shenaya, know that many hearts will travel with you to the place where his heart never left. We are all so, so sorry to have lost this lovely, courageous, Son, Brother, Father—an adventurer like no other I have ever known—my Sunshine Child—Christopher Julian. R.I.P.'

Five months after Clark's death, Barbara Clark had a fatal heart attack. Most of those who knew her were convinced that she died of a broken heart.

The family rallied around for her funeral, but disputes soon erupted in this house divided. Nasty email exchanges ensued, and some members of the family promised never to speak to other members of the family again.

Never one to relinquish control easily, Barbara Clark sent one final gift from beyond the grave. In her will, she divided her inheritance equally among her children and their descendants. All except the money that she had paid Clark two decades earlier after selling the house in Tuscany. From her 'Sunshine Child' and his children Barbara Clark deducted the £20,000 she had paid so unwillingly decades before. Barbara Clark knew how to hold a grudge.

But it was the conversations with Clark's daughters, Nicolle and Cathleen, that resonated most strongly with me. We spoke of how, even to the end, he was doing everything he could to shield those he loved from the awful truth.

'He never wanted to say how critical the situation was,' Nicolle told me. 'He never said, "I'm worried." He never said, "I'm scared." Every time, every single day, he always said, "I'm fine. I'm good. I'm okay." It was like nothing was happening. I was under shock. I still cannot realise the dynamic of events, because it was like he was on holiday.'

I never saw Clark lose control. Whether he was just keeping up appearances or something deeper lay behind it, I couldn't say. I could never tell the difference in Clark between when he was drunk and when he was sober. We'd sit there and drink six caipirinhas in a couple of hours and he'd still be just as lucid as when we'd begun. By the end, I'd just be trying to hang onto the conversation while there he was, completely in control. There was a lot happening when I was there. It was a time when the threat from Agostinho was real. But he never lost it, or admitted to fear, or thought that he might not be right. He had always been this way.

We all agreed that Clark would have hated a long, drawn-out death. There would have been nothing worse for him than to spend long months dying slowly in a British hospital. He would surely have conspired with his daughters to spring him from his prison, and together they would have fled to the Amazon. At one point they offered. But when there was no longer time left, he knew that it was time to take his leave.

'That's the first thing he said,' Nicolle agreed. '"I don't want to be a burden on anyone. I want this to be quick and for you to move on." He just decided, actually. I could tell. I knew my dad, and I saw the moment. The doctors told him, "There's not much more we can do", and he said, "Fine. That's it."'

But if Clark was ready, it was still too soon for the rest of us. He had achieved more in his shortened lifetime than many who live much longer lives. Yet we all felt that his was a life cut short. 'There's not really a good way that he could have gone away,' Nicolle said. She was, of course, right, and anyone saying otherwise was just trying to make us all feel better. 'Even if he died when he was a hundred years old, he still would have had many other things to do. My dad was one of those people who always had things to do.'

Not far beneath the surface, there was anger, the lurking suspicion that the stress and danger and betrayal of the preceding years might have driven Clark to an early grave. 'I think that Chris got sick because he got too stressed about what happened in the last ten years,' Anna Bonari told me.

Nicolle felt this especially keenly. 'I always said, "You are too kind for this world." He never wanted to admit it, but things really hurt him—about Xixuaú, about his family, about everything. He would never say, "Oh my god, I'm suffering." Never. Ever. He would always say, "I'm fine." But I know things really hurt him. He was broken. I do know it. He was not himself anymore. He wouldn't care about things in the same way, and that included himself. It has been altogether too much for him to deal with. And he never really recovered.'

His death was untimely by any measure. As Cathleen said, 'He wanted to live.'

~

And what of Xixuaú?

The Amazon in the time of COVID was one of the most desperate places on the planet. Less than a year after Clark's death, scientists estimated that an astonishing 75 per cent of the population of Manaus had had the virus. In this and other Amazonian towns, it was almost impossible not to catch it. Paul Clark and his wife Bianca, who were in Novo Airão at the time, both fell ill. Bianca nearly died. Paul couldn't return to Gaspar, because he was in dispute with Valdemar. These one-time friends and collaborators, who had founded Gaspar and had together begun an important turtle-protection project close to the village, now couldn't stand to be anywhere near each other. The virus didn't take sides. Valdemar and his wife, Socorro, both caught the virus. Socorro in particular became seriously ill due to an underlying medical condition.

Artemizia, too, became unwell, but recovered. She didn't really have a choice. As one of the few trained nurses in the Jauaperi region, she travelled tirelessly through the villages of the area, caring for the sick and administering treatment where she could. Shenaya caught the virus but her symptoms were mild. Raí, Clark's stepson, became very ill, and had a dangerously high fever for three weeks.

'Everyone has COVID,' Nicolle told me. 'Youngsters are not feeling bad, but they are going around the river travelling and fishing from one village to the other, so elders are getting sick. People keep travelling from the city to the river, so obviously it just keeps going.'

No one knew how the Waimiri-Atroari were faring. The only information I could find was that hospitals in the regional town of Rorainópolis, the closest major town north of the Waimiri-Atroari reserve, were filled with indigenous patients, most of whom had COVID.

Aside from COVID, the Rio Jauaperi was effectively closed off to outsiders and there was very little news at all leaking out of Xixuaú. From what I could glean, it had descended into a kind of anarchy, a cross between the Scar-and-hyena–led wasteland from *The Lion King* and George Orwell's *Animal Farm*. In one of my last conversations with Clark before his death, I could hear something approaching despair in voice: 'Everybody's doing whatever the hell they want. There's no law. There are no rules. People are trying to make some money because they can't go to the city.'

What seemed to upset him the most was that it was, in some cases, the children of the elders of São Pedro—those same elders who had asked him to save their world—who now hunted turtles and fished illegally at Xixuaú and in the surrounding rivers. These children had grown up with Cathleen and Nicolle.

In the months after Clark died, Nicolle, too, painted a grim picture of life in Xixuaú. 'It's burned everywhere going towards Xixuaú. When you go with the boat from Novo Airão, it's so sad right now. You just want to sit there and cry. It's nothing beautiful. It's devastating. And Xixuaú now, it's actually like a small *favela*. It's a mess. It's a total mess. It's nearly abandoned now. Only a few families live there. The families that live there, they're selling drugs, killing turtles. Imagine a house like that. My dad has been working on it all his life. Just recently, they stole Dad's boat and motors. And now they know that Artemizia's alone with the kids, they're entering basically every night to steal.'

She paused, lost in a memory.

'Xixuaú is not a good place anymore. I wouldn't want to grow up there now. If I think of Xixuaú when I was a kid— it was like paradise. If I think of what Shenaya has to go through—it's hell.'

Although unable to return, Nicolle and Cathleen were trying to find a way to get Artemizia, Shenaya and Raí to safety until the situation stabilised. 'We have to get them out of there,' she said.

'It's scary what we're going to find when all of this is over,' I ventured.

'A graveyard in the Amazon,' came Nicolle's reply.

It had indeed been a harrowing twelve months. And a lot of the news coming out of the Amazon was dispiriting at best. It seemed to herald 'the great demoralisation of the land', to borrow Conrad's memorable phrase. The situation seemed terminal.

But Clark had known many desperate moments in his time.

I was reminded of one that I learned about after his death. It was around 2008. His father was gravely ill (although he later recovered), and his marriage was not long over. Not for the first time, he stood at a crossroads. 'We still never know how it is going to end,' he wrote in his journal. 'There could be no Xixuaú reserve and community a year from now, or it could go in the opposite direction and we could be helping preserve millions of acres and guaranteeing the quality of life of hundreds of people.' He wrote of being wearied by it all, and of a growing awareness of his own mortality. And yet, 'For me and for the others it is too late to turn back and there can be no better alternative for any of us than what we have created here. Any anger, sadness, disappointment or heartbreak I suffer is compensated for by the faces of these people and the beauty of this place. It is hard to be distressed or depressed here. Nature offers one of its greatest shows on earth, twenty-four-seven and totally free.'

It had always been difficult in Xixuaú, I realised. But it was worth the struggle. And now, as then, the awful news coming out of Xixuaú wasn't the full story.

All across the Amazon, there have been widespread encroachments on indigenous lands, an acceleration of forest loss to fires and land-clearing, and much rhetoric that pushes the boundaries of what was acceptable in the Amazon. But most national parks, indigenous reserves, national forests and extractive reserves remain intact. In his first two and a half years in power, President Bolsonaro never turned his attention to Xixuaú, and most of the reserve survives in something close to its original, pristine state. Bolsonaro is up for re-election on 2 October 2022. As with Donald Trump's supporters, one can never be sure that Bolsonaro's supporters will tell pollsters their true voting intentions. Even so, the signs are that, if an election were to be held today, he would lose in a landslide.

Paul Clark is, at the time of writing, still living and working along the Jauaperi, and he continues to do important work in protecting the turtles of Xixuaú and the surrounding area. Alongside a generation of students educated in the schools in which he taught, his work in saving turtles will become his most lasting legacy.

A year after Clark's death, his daughters, Cathleen and Nicolle, were still grieving. But Nicolle managed to complete her thesis at the University of Bologna. It was a typically passionate study of Xixuaú, a study that she described to me as 'a look back to see what didn't work, so that we can actually do something in another way in the future'.

Clark had very few worldly possessions to leave his daughters. Visit Amazonia, his tourism company, was the only thing of any real value. But he left them an address book full of contacts, and the vast majority of those people worshipped their father. He also left them a place unlike anywhere else on Earth, and the story of how he had helped to save it.

If Clark were still alive, he could have reminded everyone that he, too, had spent much of his life weathering near-catastrophic storms, that there were many times when all hope seemed lost. This cultured man with the guile and sensibility of a street fighter had always understood the importance of the long-term view. Throughout his life he had displayed an unfathomable capacity to deflect disappointments. And he had possessed a clear-eyed ability to absorb his former enemies into the cause. He also knew how to turn apparent defeat into a source of strength: as that Brazilian politician once told Clark and his merry men, in a phrase they never forgot, 'The more we batter you, the stronger you become.' He knew there was no final defeat. He never gave up.

Perhaps this was why, in the months before his death, he had begun negotiating with the city of Coventry in England, which suffered widespread destruction after being heavily bombed during WWII, for a partnership with Xixuaú. I can see him smiling at the symbolism of a city that rose, reborn, from the ashes, pairing with a natural wonder under fire. Had he lived, he would have rolled up his sleeves and got back to work.

We will never know for sure, but I imagine that Clark would have viewed his own death through nature's prism of ruthless cause and effect. He would have understood his passing in the context of the constant struggle for life in the jungle. When talking with Ben Fogle in 2018, Clark spoke of the never-ending battle against termites which, if left unchecked, would devour everything. Fogle asked if that was symbolic of life in the Amazon.

'In a way it is. Everything is rushing to grow, rushing to eat, rushing to survive, and then dying quickly, and then the next generation comes along. It's very fast out here in the forest.'

Back in 2008, he had wondered in his journal whether his early death 'might actually forward our cause'. Writing of himself and his brother Paul, he said, 'We might be in the situation of being able to go to our final rest without winning our war and then it might be won afterwards, helped by this fact . . . Pass the torch. There are people who could carry it to its destination.'

One day, when it is safe for them to do so, Cathleen and Nicolle will return to Xixuaú. They will carry Clark's ashes with them. They will take him home. Together, they will mourn with Artemizia and Shenaya and Raí. In time, they will resume a conversation that began in 1990, from a time before any of them was born. In time, they will start talking about how to save Xixuaú.

I can picture the scene as they sit by the water, telling stories about Clark, talking about what needs to be done. The gilded light on the forest canopy. The pink dolphins rising and falling like waves on still waters. The mystery of toucans and jaguars and giant otters.

Out there in Xixuaú, in spite of everything, the dawn still feels like Earth's first morning.

# Acknowledgements

I will always be thankful that I had the opportunity to spend time with Chris Clark in Xixuaú, and that he told me his story. He was a remarkable man. This book is dedicated to his memory.

I am extremely grateful to Chris Clark's family and friends who took the time to speak with me and share their stories of Chris and of Xixuaú. Special thanks to Nicolle and Cathleen Clark, Paul Clark, Anna Bonari, Valdemar, Artemizia, Lady Madeleine Kleinwort, Tom Haycraft and others.

To everyone at Allen & Unwin, heartfelt thanks. I feel privileged to have Jane Palfreyman in my corner: no author could wish for a wiser and more supportive publisher. Thanks also to the wonderful Samantha Kent and Emma Driver for expert editing and taking such care over the manuscript, and to Isabelle O'Brien and Rebecca Richards-Hill for their boundless publicity expertise.

I am grateful as ever to Michael Dreelan, Nick Lenaghan, Pam Newton, Peter Stockman and so many others for being such faithful readers of my first book. Thanks to Lisa, Alex, Greta and Greg for their support, and for having more copies of the book in one home than anyone else. And I remain humbled by the ongoing support and kindness shown to me by Wouter Vergeer, Alan Murphy, Matthijs Verberkmoes, Jeroen Beekwilder and everyone at SafariBookings: they're the reason that I am still able to earn my living as a writer.

To my family, eternal thanks. Marina has been my love and life partner for the past two decades and all the world has been our home. I wouldn't change a thing. When it comes to my daughters, Carlota and Valentina, I so often find myself lost for words. I am so proud of them and I love every minute of their company. Reach for the stars, my loves, and smash the patriarchy while you're at it. I miss my father, Ron, every day. He was my biggest fan, and a good man. My mother Jan is the best person I know. She came up with the title of this book. She has always been my moral compass. And she's the one who taught me to look beyond the horizon.

# Notes

1   Two hundred Brazilian reais is equivalent to about 50 Australian dollars.
2   A small ship with three masts used in the fifteenth and sixteenth centuries, especially by the Portuguese and the Spanish.
3   The use of the term 'Indian' throughout this book and in other sources is problematic. The name was given to the Indigenous inhabitants of South and Central America by early European explorers because the explorers believed that they had arrived in India. Although its use has often been pejorative, I have used it in preference to other formulations, including 'Native Americans' (which can be confused with the First Nations peoples of North America), because 'Indians' (or, rather, '*Indios*') is widely used throughout Brazil, including by Indigenous people themselves and their supporters.
4   IBAMA is an agency within the Brazilian Ministry of the

Environment and is Brazil's primary environmental body. It implements and polices the federal government's environmental policies.

5   This is the equivalent of approximately 5000 square kilometres.

# About the Author

Anthony Ham is one of Australia's most experienced nature and travel writers. For more than two decades, he has been travelling to the earth's wild places in search of stories, to Africa, the Amazon, the Arctic, and Outback Australia. His work has appeared in *The New York Times*, *Smithsonian Magazine*, *National Geographic Traveler*, *BBC Travel*, *The Age*, *The Sydney Morning Herald*, *The Monthly*, *Virginia Quarterly Review (VQR)*, *BBC Wildlife*, *Lonely Planet Traveller*, *Africa Geographic*, *The Independent*, *Travel Africa*, and elsewhere. Through his writing, Anthony's readers have observed up close Africa's most endangered elephant herd, travelled to remove villages behind al-Qaeda lines, and experienced the beginnings of Libya's long descent into chaos. Anthony has also written or co-written more than 135 travel guides for Lonely Planet, including *Brazil*. He believes in the power of the written word, the enduring powers of stories, and the importance of writing beautifully about important things. His first book, *The Last Lions of Africa*, was published by Allen & Unwin in 2020. He lives in Melbourne with his wife and two children.

www.anthonyham.com